DACIA
THE ROMAN WARS

VOLUME I

SARMIZEGETUSA

Text & Illustrations
RADU OLTEAN

KARWANSARAY PUBLISHERS
THE NETHERLANDS — 2014

Acknowledgements: Dan Dimăncescu, Valeriu Sârbu, Anișoara Sion, Matei Florian Popescu, Iosif Vasile Ferencz, Daniel Spânu, Cătălin Borangic, Gabriela Gheorghiu, Costea Florea, Alexandru Berzovan, Andrei Mihai, Lucrezia Ungaro, Cătălina Macovei, Leonard Velcescu, Bogdan Condurățeanu, Alina Popescu, Aurora Pețan, Dan Oltean, Mihai Cârstăian, Coriolan Opreanu, Tudor Berza, Codrin Bucur, Melania Cristina Cotoi, Cristian Lascu, Monica Mărgineanu Cârstoiu, Horea Pop, Vitalie Bârcă, Ovidiu Țentea, Carmen Bem, Liviu Petculescu, Melinda Mitu, Ana Gruia, Cristina Stanciu, Kyle Brandse, Michael Tran, Frederik Marmann, Alexandra Carlsson, Nora Agapi, Ronnie Otero, Dan Marino, Ionuț Macri, Ciprian Udrescu, Sandra Ecobescu și Fundația Calea Victoriei, Marin Neagoe, Dragoș Mândescu, Alexandru Skultety, Andrei Gonciar, Cristina Mitar, Marius Barbu, Paul Cheptea and reenactment group Terra Dacica Aeterna, Răzvan Mateescu, Cristi Roman, Gelu Florea .

Special thanks to Ernest Oberländer-Târnoveanu, the General Director of the Romanian National History Museum (MNIR-București), and his colleagues Cornel Constantin Ilie, George Nica and Mihai Bozgan, who offered me their generous support and enabled me to publish photographs of valuable museum artifacts.

All my gratitude to the Stamp Bureau of the Romanian Academy Library (BAR), the National History Museum of Transylvania (MNIT), the Orăștie History and Ethnography Museum, National History and Archaeology Museum in Constanța (MINA), the Deva Museum of Dacian and Roman Civilization (MCDR), the Huniad Castle Museum in Hunedoara and the museums in Rome mentioned in the book.

PROOF READING: Cătălin Borangic, Domnica Macri
TRANSLATION: Domnica Macri
DESIGN: Radu Oltean, Dragoș Oltean
ARCHITECTURE RECONSTRUCTION CONSULTANT: Anișoara Sion, Architect
HISTORY AND ARCHAEOLOGY CONSULTANTS: Valeriu Sârbu, Matei Florian Popescu, Daniel Spânu, Iosif Vasile Ferencz, Cătălin Borangic, Alexandru Berzovan, Andrei Mihai

Most illustrations of scenes from Trajan's Column were based on casts at the National History Museum in Bucharest.

Published by KARWANSARAY PUBLISHERS, ROTTERDAM, THE NETHERLANDS - 2014
ISBN 978-94-90258-11-5

KARWANSARAY PUBLISHERS B.V.
Phone: +31-575-776076
E-mail: service@karwansaraypublishers.com

Page 3: Trajan and Decebalus. Detail from a 5,000 lei banknote issued in 1945
Page 5: Aerial view of terraces in the Sacred Area, Grădiştea Muncelului archaeological site, taken in March 2011. Photo: Nicholas Dimăncescu

Foreword

This book offers a fresh view on the Dacian-Roman wars. I have gathered and adapted archeological findings and historical studies, old and new, for a wider public of history lovers. I have tried to avoid too much speculation on events that remain unclear. On occasion, I have ventured to offer possible scenarios for the rare instances when historical or archaeological sources were more generous. What is shared in this book is my attempt to come closer to the historical truth.

I should add that in my book the word barbarian does not carry the current meaning of "rude, uncivilized", but is used in its Greek sense of "foreigner," i.e. someone who spoke an incomprehensible language. Barbarians are therefore simply peoples outside Greco-Roman culture.

This book is addressed to the general public and that is why it does not follow all the rules of academic quotation. The authors whose ideas, opinions and research were used are mentioned in the bibliography at the end of the book.

Radu Oltean
April 2013

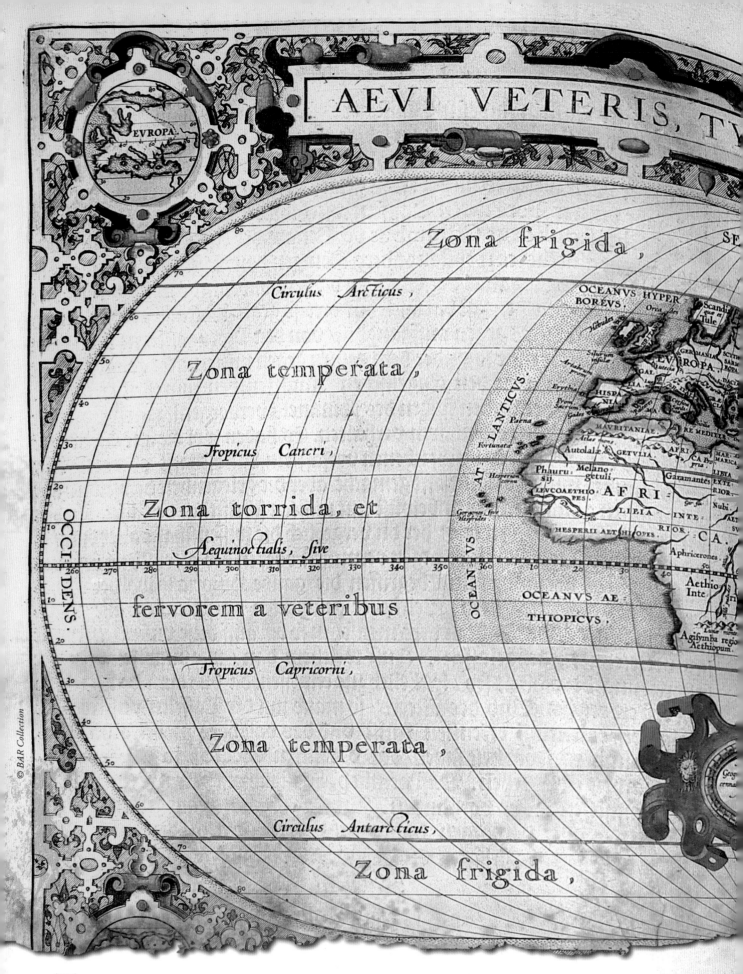

There was a time when the world appeared much smaller than we might imagine it today. And that was because people knew so little of it. Ancient Europeans such as Greeks, Celts, Romans, Thracians, Iberians and numerous northern populations each imagined their land as the center of the world. Their worlds – larger for some, smaller for others – stretched only as far as their geographical

GEOGRAPHICVS.

ASIA.

et inhabitabilis.

Sive Borealis.

et habitabilis.

Sive Aestivalis.

ob Solis nimium

Aequidialis circulus.

inhabitabilis credita.

Sive Hyemalis.

et habitabilis.

Sive Australis.

et inhabitabilis.

SCYTHIA EXTRA IMAVM.
SCYTHIA INTRA IMAVM.
SINARVM REGIO
ASIA
SACAE
SERICA
BACTRIANA
Taurus mons.
Corancali.
INDIA EXTRA GANGEM.
Cudutar.
INDIA INTRA GANGEM.
Sinus Magnus
Sinus Gangeticus.
TAPROBANA
MARE RVBRVM.
MARE EOVM.
INDICVS OCEANVS.

ORIENS.

boundaries. On a beautiful map etched by Dutch cartographer Abraham Ortelius in 1590, during the age of great geographic awakening, one sees the World as described by Europeans and Middle Easterners at the end of the Antiquity. But much earlier during the 2nd century AD, the center of the world was in Rome, the capital of its largest, richest and most powerful Empire.

Temple of *Jupiter Optimus Maximus Capitolinus*

Capitoline Hill

Old, republican Forum

Caesar's Forum

Forum Transitorium (of Nerva)

Forum of Peace (of Vespasian)

ROME

We are in the center of Rome, on an October day in 117 AD. Citizens are in mourning as they take part in the funeral of a man known as *"optimus princeps"* – the highest of princes. This is *Imperator Caesar Nerva Traianus Augustus* (official name) who died at age 65 two months earlier returning from a campaign in Asia Minor against the Parthians. Inflicted by a partial paralysis, probably after a stroke, he succumbed on August 9th at Selinus (today's Gazipasha, Turkey) in the province of Cilicia. Later, the town would be renamed Traianopolis and a monumental cenotaph (empty grave) would be erected there in his memory. Trajan's body was taken to Seleucia (today's Selefke, Turkey) and cremated. An urn aboard a sailing ship having carried his ashes to Rome, he would be ceremoniously interred within the base of the Column

Trajan's
Forum

Trajan's Market

Augustus's
Forum

already dedicated to his memory four years earlier. Let's take a look at this central part of the city. It's the area of the *fora*, surrounding the Capitoline Hill where stand the Romans' most sacred temples. The most important of them is the Temple of *Jupiter Optimus Maximus Capitolinus*, recently reconstructed by Emperor Domitian after a fire in 80 AD. At the foot of the Hill stands the Old Forum from the republican period.

The idea of imperial *fora* sponsored by Emperors originated with Julius Caesar and continued with Augustus. In the valley between the Quirinal and the Capitoline Hill, five such grandiose complexes were erected by Caesar, Vespasian (the Peace Forum), Nerva (most of it built by Domitian) and now Trajan.

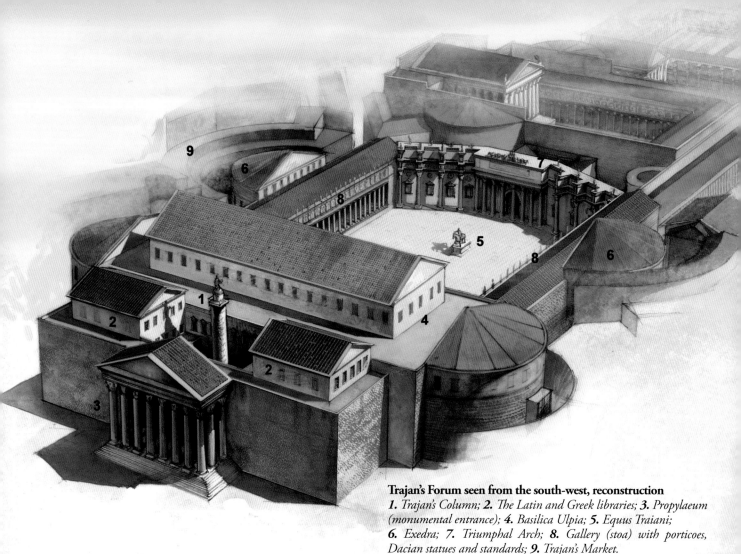

Trajan's Forum seen from the south-west, reconstruction
1. Trajan's Column; 2. The Latin and Greek libraries; 3. Propylaeum (monumental entrance); 4. Basilica Ulpia; 5. Equus Traiani; 6. Exedra; 7. Triumphal Arch; 8. Gallery (stoa) with porticoes, Dacian statues and standards; 9. Trajan's Market.

THE FORUM

Trajan's Forum was inaugurated in 112 AD at the western extremity of the Hill – the last and most magnificent forum ever built in Rome. It took six years to build since a second victorious expedition against Decebalus, the Dacian king. It covered 6 hectares (15 acres) of land – so much that excavations into the flank of the Quirinal Hill initiated by Domitian had to be continued.

Designed by great architect Apollodorus of Damascus, the Forum surpassed all others in size. A huge plaza covered in marble was surrounded by colonnaded porticoes; a basilica rose at one end with a huge marble hall supported by three rows of columns and apses on the short

Apollodorus of Damascus
Roman bust from the collection of the Glyptothek in Munich, Germany.

sides; two libraries were added; and most unusually for the times, a commemorative column towered at one end; the whole was entered through two monumental access ways.

In the middle of the vast plaza rose a colossal gold-covered bronze statue of Emperor Trajan astride his horse – *Equus Traiani*. Records mention it still standing in late 4th century. In present days only a humble piece of marble from its base remains, recently discovered by Italian archaeologists. The south-eastern entrance to the Forum was a triumphal arch, with a bronze statue of victorious Trajan in a six-horse chariot, while the north-western entrance was a monumental *propylaeum* decorated with huge Egyptian granite columns.

The magnificent complex was built in expensive colored stone shipped in from Asia Minor, Greece or Egypt. Behind the basilica, the two symmetrical libraries were meant to host the Imperial Archives – one the Latin documents and the other, the Greek ones.

Between the library buildings, in a small inner court, the Column rose. Its bas-relief sculptures could be seen from the terraces specially created on the libraries and basilica. The artifacts decorating the whole ensemble commemorated the conquest of Dacia and glorified Trajan's deeds and indomitable army. The complex hosted official ceremonies and displayed statues of public personalities. Within the basilica a tribunal presided over slave-freeing ceremonies. These were previously carried out at the *Atrium Libertatis,* which had to be demolished to make way for the Forum

Trajan's Market. Deeply dug into the western slope of the Quirinal, for space, a huge commercial area was created, known today as Trajan's Market. The works had been started by Domitian, Trajan's predecessor, and were completed at the same time as the Forum, to which the market was connected. It was built on three terraces carved into the flank of the Hill and had a semicircular shape because it included the *exedra* of Trajan's Forum. Most buildings there were for commercial use: shops, warehouses, offices.

Dacian statues. Everything in Trajan's Forum was designed to glorify the Emperor and Rome's Legions. References to the Dacian Wars were obsessively displayed. If you stood by the colossal golden equestrian statue at the center and looked up and around, you would have been awed by the many dozens of Dacian warriors standing mute in finely carved marble, amidst trophies and military standards of the legions who had taken part in the Dacian Wars. Among the commemorative texts and the names of military units inscribed on the monuments, the words *ex manubiis* were also found. They meant built with proceeds from the booty taken by soldiers. It was thus that the Forum was financed from the spoils of war in Dacia.

On the attic, above each column of the lateral portico, stood a captive Dacian or, alternately, a decorated marble shield (named *clipei*). The façade of the basilica also displayed Dacian statues alternating with huge reliefs of piles of weapons like those on the base of the column and of Trajan's equestrian statue. How did these monuments look like 1,900 years ago? Two of the reconstruction versions are illustrated here. One belongs to Italian scholars who deduced that two rows of Dacian statues were arrayed, although that would bring the number of statues to at least 200. Another belongs to the American Professor James Parker, who concluded from his own exhaustive research that only one row of Dacian statues decorated the attic, while the battlement was embellished by bronze copies of the military standards. According to him, there must have been around 60 to 80 Dacian statues decorating the top of the Forum of which there were two types. In two sizes of 2.6 and 3 meters (8.5 and 10 feet), some were simple, carved in white marble, while others included two types of stone: colored (*pavonazzeto*) for the body and clothing and white for the head and hands.

What one sees today are Dacian statues brought from other monuments in Trajan's or Hadrian's time, from Rome or elsewhere, as well as from destroyed monuments erected by Domitian. Some are copies made as

Dacian statues from Trajan's Forum
Two reconstructed versions of the lateral porticoes.
Details in the text.

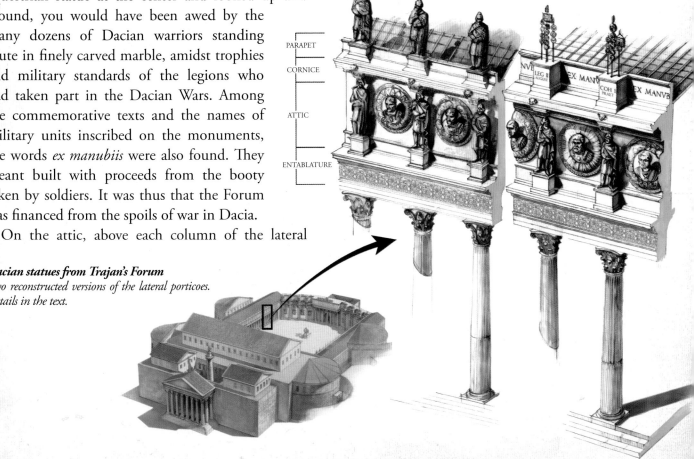

late as the 18ᵗʰ century. It must be said that not all Roman statues representing bearded men with trousers and caps (*pilei*) were of Dacians. Many were of Parthians. Their representation at the time was very similar and statues (now widely scattered in museums) are hard to differentiate when it is no longer clear what monument they came from.

Decorating monuments with statues of enslaved barbarians was not new in Roman architecture. But unseen before Trajan's Forum was both the sheer number and the remarkable respect shown for the Dacian prisoners – given our own contemporary mindset of discrediting the loser in battle. What could have been the explanation for Trajan's attitude towards the Dacian vanquished? His predecessor Emperor Domitian's equestrian statue, known only from coins, displayed the horse with a

Dacian heads at the Vatican
Two heads of Dacian prisoners (a **comat***, on the left, and a* **pileat***) are exhibited at the Vatican Museum in Rome. Originally, they belonged to Dacian statues of the Forum. Completed and restored in the 19ᵗʰ century, they only partially retain their original aspect. Modern insertions are highlighted in color on the right.*

hoof atop a severed Dacian head. Marcus Aurelius' column shows no goodwill towards the vanquished Germans shown in humiliating postures, brutalized, massacred. This is totally opposite to Dacians as depicted in the Forum and on Trajan's Column,

Dacian statues from Trajan's Forum. *The first two on the left are in* pavonazzetto *marble; they had their head and hands sculpted separately in white marble. Note the hollow between the shoulders, where the head was fixed. On the right, a Dacian statue in white marble.* Museo dei Fori Imperiali, *Rome.*

Heads of Dacian noblemen, wearing the specific cap, pileus, in white marble. Original from Trajan's Forum. Note the shape of the cap, with the small, flat tip.
Left and center: *storage at* Fornici del Teatro del Marcello, *photo: Leonard Velcescu;*
Right*: storage at* Museo dei Fori Imperiali, *Rome.*

though bloody scenes are present. By showing his captured enemies unchained and in resigned but dignified poses, was Trajan boasting the virtues of a victor in front of the Roman people? Was he thus not just the paragon of courage, bravery and justice, but also of *clementia* and *humanitas*? Mercy, tolerance and respect for human dignity (including that of conquered enemies) were among the qualities that Trajan had indeed to possess in his quality as *optimus princeps* – a title bestowed upon him by the Senate and minted on his coins.

If Roman propaganda and perception of Dacians was largely negative in 101 AD, before the conquest of Dacia, after 106 the dramatic battles and the heroism of the Dacians impressed their Roman contemporaries. These feared enemies, whose valor as fighters was confirmed by the statues of the Forum and by the two costly wars required to see them defeated, became a symbol of Rome's might. Their status, according to official propaganda, was not that of a conquered people but, rather, that of future citizens absorbed into the Empire. This is the message one can read in Trajan's monuments. But this is only true for Rome, the capital city.

At the frontiers of the Empire, things were different. On Tropaeum Traiani, in Scythia Minor, the attitude towards conquered barbarians was neither magnanimous nor friendly (see the chapter on the Adamclisi monument). King Decebalus' death by his own hand, to avoid being dragged into slavery by his victors, was considered as a heroic and dignified end

that impressed the people of the time. Sympathy for Decebalus and the Dacian people is left for us to read in a letter sent by Pilny the Younger, who was close to Trajan, to the poet Caninius Rufus who set out to pen a poem about the Dacian war.

"I greatly approve your design of writing a poem upon the Dacian war. For where could you have chosen a subject so new, so full of events, so extensive, and so poetical? A subject which while it has all the marvels of fiction, has all the solidity of truth. You will sing of rivers turned into new channels, and rivers bridged for the first time, of camps pitched upon craggy mountains, and of a king superior to adversity, though forced to abandon his capital city and even his life. You will describe, too, the victor's double triumph, one of which [102 AD] was the first that was ever gained over that nation, till then unsubdued, as the other was the final. I foresee only one difficulty, but that one is serious ; to make the style equal to the grandeur of the subject is a vast and arduous undertaking even for your genius ". (The letter of Pliny the Younger to Caninius Rufus. English translation by William Melmoth, revised By W. M. L. Hutchinson, "Pliny Letters", The Loeb Classical Library)

From this excerpt, it is easier to grasp what Romans thought of the Dacians and about Decebalus. By subduing a courageous and indomitable foe, by the unusual sacrifices made by the Roman army to depose them, and by the dignified presentation of a vanquished enemy, Rome glorified its own strength.

CONSTANTINE'S ARCH

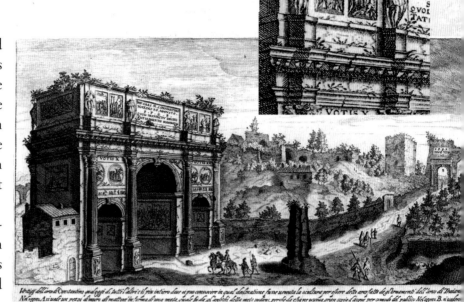

Built in the 4th century and preserved to this day, the monument was dedicated by the Senate and the people of Rome to Constantine I (the Great, 306-337) in 315, to mark ten years of reign – *deccenalia* – and the victory in the Battle of the Milvian Bridge (28th of October, 312) against the usurper Maxentius.

Additional sculpted decorations were mostly recovered from older monuments from the times of Domitian, Trajan, Hadrian and Marcus Aurelius.

Constantine's Arch in the 1740s. *Note the Dacian statues restored in 1733. Etching by Giovanni Battista Piranesi, 18th century. BAR Collection.*

Constantine's Arch today. *Detail of two Dacian statues on the eastern side of the monument.*
Bottom left: *Statue of Dacian prisoner in pavonazzetto marble, with head and hands reconstructed in the 18th century.*

The only sculpture made especially for this arch was the frieze depicting Constantine's military campaigns, surrounding the construction like a belt. On the attic, above each of the eight columns, were Dacians' statues, almost certainly taken from Trajan's Forum and exhibited in a very similar setting.

All eight statues were carved from two types of marble. The clothing was in colored marble, yellow with violent veins (*pavonazzeto*, from Asia Minor), while the arms and heads were made out of white marble. These parts were mostly destroyed over centuries when, in 1530, Lorenzino di Pierfrancesco de' Medici from Florence cut the heads of the Dacian statues and had to flee the city to escape punishment. The episode brought him the nickname of "Lorenzaccio the head-cutter". For 200 years, the statues on Constantine's Arch remained headless.

Only in 1732-1733, at the request of Pope Clementius XII, would sculptor Pietro Bracci restore the heads and hands of seven statues, while an eighth, crushed in a fall, was replaced by a copy[1].

---

1 Ironically, this replica is frequently offered as an example of what ancient statues of Dacians looked like.

THE GREAT TRAJANIC FRIEZE

Both sides of the Arch of Constantine and the inner walls of the main arch are decorated with four huge scenes of battle between Romans and Dacians, moved here from other monuments. Historians named them the Great Trajanic Frieze. The frieze includes the portrait of an Emperor, re-crafted to resemble Constantine. What appears certain is that it was first meant to commemorate one of the two Dacian campaigns between 101 and 106 AD. It survived broken in four pieces and provides valuable information on the military equipment of both sides.

A cast replica of the four fragments placed side by side is kept at the Roman Civilization Museum in Rome. Judging by the ornaments of the shields, featuring the scorpion, and by the feathered helmets, most Roman soldiers are most likely from the Praetorian Guard. The Dacians are shown as completely crushed by an attack of the Praeto-

rian Cavalry led by the Emperor. They are depicted as dead, in agony or committing suicide. A Dacian leader throws himself at the feet of the Emperor asking for mercy, while the severed heads of four other warlords are presented to him by his Legionaries.

As background scenery, two circular wooden (or reed?) houses can be seen.

Top: *Detail on the northern frieze of Constantine's Arch, Rome. On the right foreground, a Dacian warrior with a short curved sword.*

Bottom: *The Great Trajanic Frieze, reconstructed by placing the casts of the four scenes side by side. Museo della Civiltà Romana, Rome.*

The southern frieze of Constantine's Arch. *Roman cavalry attack led by the Emperor (see reconstructed image). Riders trample the Dacians on the sound of battle horns. The aggressive and spiteful attitude towards the vanquished indicates that this work likely belongs to Domitian's period.*

Top left: *Etching by Nicolas Beatrizet, 1553. BAR Collection.*

Bottom: *The same frieze, today.*

TRAJAN'S COLUMN

Let's go back to the ceremonial event in the fall of 117 AD. The Empire is now ruled by Hadrian, whom Trajan adopted two days before he died on August 9th that year. The late Emperor's faithful wife, Plotina, leads he funerary cortege. A massive gold urn carrying Trajan's ashes is placed in a small chamber at the base of the Column. There being no funerary monument yet constructed, the Roman senate agreed on the Column as the most appropriate tomb, one memorializing the terrible events of the Dacian wars

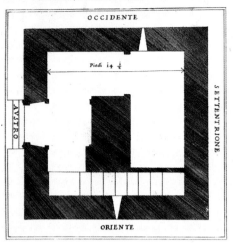

Pianta interna, et esterna del Piedestallo

OCCIDENTE

Piedi 14 ½

AVSTRO

SETTENTRIONE

ORIENTE

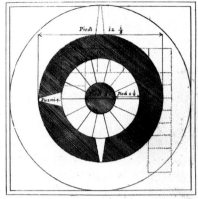

Pianta dell'ingresso, con la Scala lumaca della Colonna.

Piedi 12 ½

Piedi 4

Piedi 2 ¼

Anima della lumaca piedi 3. di diametro.
Gradini lunghi piedi 2 ½.

Trajan's Column

Left: *A reconstruction of Trajan's funeral in October 117.*
Top: *Plan of the base and spindle and vertical sections.*
Bottom: *The funerary room and the interior structure of the Column.*
Etchings from the album **Colonna Traiana** *by Pietro Santi Bartoldi, late 17ᵗʰ century.*

Statua di S·Pietro

Piedi 13

Base della Statua

Piedi 8

Piedi 9 ⅙

Piedestallo con la Cimasa

Piedi 8 ½

Piedi 14 ¼

Capitello

Piedi 4

Piedi 10 ½

Diametro di sopra della Colonna piedi 10 ½

Il Piede della Colonna ha ½ diametro piedi 12 ½

Base, cioe il plinto co toro.

Guscio

Cornice

Piedestallo

Base del Piedestallo

Dado

Piedi 21.

Annotationi di Alfonso Ciaccone

Questo segno ✻ e posto per noia di quello, che si e aggiunto, e corretto

LA COLONNA TRAIANA fu dedicata dal Senato, e Popolo Romano all'Imp. Traiano nel suo Foro in Roma, per opera di Apollodoro Architetto.

Nella sua esteriore circonferenza si vede scolpita di bassorilievo tutta la Guerra Dacica, la prima, e la seconda Espeditione contro il Rè Decebalo.

SENATVS·POPVLVSQVE·ROMANVS
IMP·CAESARI·DIVI·NERVAE·F·NERVAE
TRAIANO·AVG·GERM·DACICO·PONTIF
MAXIMO·TRIB·POT·XVII·IMP·VI·COS·VI·PP
AD·DECLARANDVM·QVANTAE·ALTITVDINIS
MONS·ET·LOCVS·TANT···RIBVS·SIT·EGESTVS

Pedestal at the base of Trajan's Column. *The side with the entrance and the inscription.*
The carving above the door was made in the early Middle Ages. Etching by Giovanni Battista Piranesi, 18ᵗʰ century. BAR Colection.

in detailed bas-reliefs highlighted in brilliant colors.

Inaugurated on the 12ᵗʰ of May in 113 AD, a year after the Forum, the Column was like none before and in time became an inspiration for many others, from Marc Aurelius' column in Rome to that of Arcadius in Constantinople and to Napoleon's in Place Vendôme, Paris. It impressed its contemporaries and remains a source of fascination, both in terms of engineering and of artistic expression. The column is shaped like an oversized Doric column on a cubic pedestal, with an enormous laurel crown around its base. The huge marble tower was erected out of 19 drum-shape blocks weighing over 30 metric tons each (33 tons US), precisely positioned one on top of the other. They had slightly different diameters (3.83-3.66 meters or about 12 feet) in order to provide an optical

Trajan's Column today. *View from the roof of a neighboring building. The granite columns of the Basilica Ulpia are visible behind the Column. Photo: Kyle Brandse.*

correction of the perspective, according to designs the Greeks had discovered centuries before. So basically the column resembles a spindle, slightly bulging at the middle. It is hard to imagine the intricate pulley system engineers used for this construction. The works were coordinated by Apollodorus of Damascus who integrated the monument into the design of the entire Forum complex. Without the statue on the top, the column rose to almost 40 meters (130 feet). At the bottom, a door opened into a vestibule which let to a spiral stair well. Above stood a huge golden bronze statue representing Trajan, replacing what was initially a bronze eagle. An inscription in finely chiseled letters crowned the door.

"THE SENATE AND PEOPLE OF ROME (erected this monument) TO THE EMPEROR CAESAR NERVA TRAJAN AUGUSTUS, SON OF NERVA, OF BLESSED MEMORY, CONQUEROR IN GERMANY AND DACIA, HIGH PRIEST, VESTED WITH THE TRIBUNICIAN POWER 17 TIMES, PROCLAIMED IMPERATOR (honorary title meaning supreme commander and victor) 6 TIMES, ELECTED CONSUL 6 TIMES, TO THE FATHER OF THE NATIONS: AS AN ILLUSTRATION OF THE HEIGHT WHICH THIS HILL AND PLACE ATTAINED, NOW REMOVED FOR SUCH GREAT WORKS AS THESE."

The accounts depicted in bas-relief that wrap upward like a spiral ribbon were inspired by Trajan's *Commentaries*, a sort of diary similar to the one Julius Caesar wrote during his Gallic wars. They describe the two war campaigns against Dacian King Decebalus and his tribal allies in the lower Danube River region. At some point, Trajan's writings were lost and the column reliefs are the only reminders. Unfurled, they would stretch 200 meters (660 feet) and count over 2,500 sculpted individuals. Trajan appears at least twenty times; Decebalus five or six. Teams of stone workers, probably Greek and the best of their times, created one of the most lauded bas-reliefs in Roman art. Modern-day surface examinations under fluorescent

A pile of Dacian and Sarmatian weapons sculpted on one side of the Column.
A photo overlapped on an etching by G.B. Piranesi shows the precision of the Italian master.

1. *Bucca fatta scavare da Sisto V. con recinto
di muro, e Scala, che discende al piano della Colonna.*

Colonna Trajana

2. *Chiesa del Nome di Maria.*   Piranesi
3. *Palazzo Bonelli.*
Presso l'autore a Strada Felice nel Palazzo Tomati vicino alla Trinità de'monti. A paoli due e mezzo

Detail from the Column. The Battle of Tapae. Photo taken in 2011.

light hinted at vivid colors once animating the bas-reliefs. Subsequent attempts at color reconstruction are purely hypothetical. Many of the weapons carried by characters on the frieze were painted, but some, especially spears, were made of copper and fixed into their fists. The Column stood in a small courtyard surrounded by colonnades, which led to the libraries and to Basilica Ulpia (see the reconstruction of the Forum). Some historians claim that the reliefs were added during Hadrian, Trajan's successor and adoptive son, who also took part in the Dacian wars. The theory was based on the coins minted by Trajan, showing the Column without any decorations. During the first Christian centuries, when pagan monuments in Rome were abandoned to decay, two small churches were built next to the Column. They practically saved the monument, which was officially "adopted" by the church at the end of the 16th century. It was then completely unearthed (the base had been buried) and Pope Sixtus V ordered a bronze statue of St. Peter by Gerolamo della Porta to be placed on its top, where Trajan's statue had once stood (and whence it had vanished in the Middle Ages, in unknown circumstances). Trajan's Column is the only part of the Forum to withstand the millennia nearly intact.

Above: *Aureus (Roman gold coin) with a representation of the Column.*

Right: *Reconstruction of the Column as it probably looked when it was completed.*

THE NORTHERN THRACIANS

The written history of Northern Thrace[1] starts with the first mention of the Getae by Herodotus at the end of the 6th century BC, during the expedition of Persian king Darius against the Scythians, and ends with the decimation of Decebalus' kingdom[2] by Emperor Trajan after the campaigns of 101-102 and 105-106 AD. Modern historians have split these 600 years of history in three. From about 500 to 250 BC, the classical Getae civilization develops around the Lower Danube bounded by the Balkan Mountains, the Carpathian Mountains and the Black Sea. This was the time, contemporary to the Greek classical and Hellenistic civilization, famed for its gold and silver treasures, the royal tombs in Sveshtari (in northern Bulgaria, near Isperih), and the rule of king Dromichaites.

The second period between 250 and 125 BC, more difficult to decipher, included major changes as the Celts and their civilization reached what is

Royal Dacian gold bracelet no. 13. *Weight: 933.4 grams. Discovered by archaeological poachers in 2001 on Grădiștea Muncelului Hill, alongside five other similar bracelets. Romanian authorities recovered them in 2011 from the international antiquities market. Photo: Marius Amarie. © - MNIR București.*

present-day Transylvania between the 4th and the early 3rd centuries. *"Starting with the 3rd century, an interesting phenomenon took place between the north-western Balkans and Transylvania. Archaeologists speak about a slow migration (perhaps withdrawal) covering at least three generation of warrior tribes. These groups had different ethnic origins and religions, displayed elements of*

---

1 Comprising the later tribes of the Triballi and Moesi, who were close to the Getae.

2 On the fringes of Roman Dacia, various Dacian barbarian tribes would persist. Historians named them "free Dacians", among which best known were the Carpi and the Costoboci. They would not rise to the levels of culture reached by classic Dacian civilization in the Burebistas-Decebalus period.

Royal Dacian gold bracelet no. 13, detail. *One of the tips of the bracelet above. This type of golden bracelets were probably buried as offerings to the gods by royalty in Sarmizegetusa, the only place where they were discovered. They were made of alluvial gold from the Metaliferi Mountain Range in Transylvania. Silver versions of the bracelets were discovered over a wider range, including Wallachia and occasionally Bulgaria and Serbia. They are typical only from the 1st century BC. Note the skill of the goldsmith, who shaped the metal while cold. Mineral deposits are visible in the grooves. Photo: Marius Amarie. © - MNIR București.*

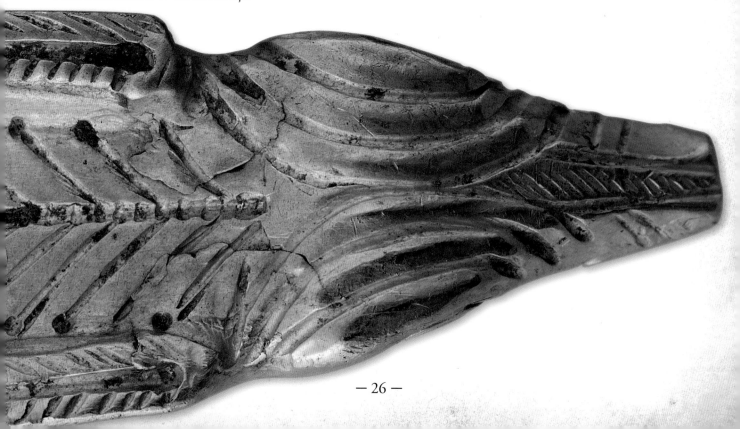

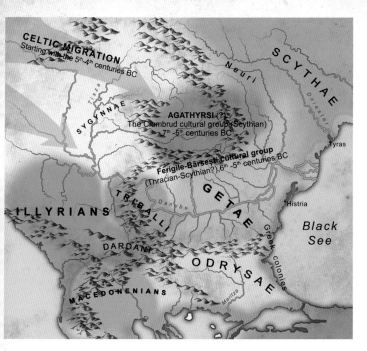
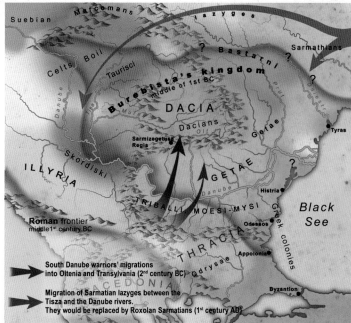

Eastern Europe, the Balkans, the Lower Danube Region and the Carpathian Range in ancient times
Left: *6th - 4th centuries BC.*
Right: *2nd -1st centuries BC, as it was before and during Burebista's Kingdom (ca 70 - 44 BC).*
The late migration of Sarmatian Iazyges (1st century AD) is also represented.

Celtic and Thracian culture, but shared common interests, strategies and tactics. The movement seems to have been generated by the growing influence of the Roman Empire in the Balkan Peninsula[3].

Crossing the Danube into today's Oltenia in southern Romania, these groups, led by an elite of professional warriors, absorbed the Getae, who were at the peak of their power. One or two generations later, they were consolidated a greater Dacian state by King Burebistas" (Cătălin Borangic).[4] These southern warriors contributed to the disappearance of the Celts long settled in Transylvania and established the Dacian civilization centered within a mountainous Carpathian region with Sarmizegetusa as the seat of power.

The last of the three periods, the high-point of Dacian power, lasted from about 125 BC to 106 AD constitutes the principal focus of this book. It was a time of wealth-accumulation for the Dacians triggering many social, political, religious and cultural changes. Under King Burebistas around 82-44 BC, the previously divided warring tribes of northern Dacians and of the southern Getae, themselves influenced by Greek culture, were united for the first time.
Among the religious changes, one is worth mentioning:

the disappearance of necropoleis for commoners.[5] At the same time, the aristocracy embraced burial rituals by incineration and human sacrifices became more frequent .[6] As a result and until the Roman conquest, modern-day archeologists face a void of burial grounds lasting for more than 200 years.

Other signs of the Dacians' radical spiritual transformations in the last century BC were the large worship centers aligned with sacred mountain sites like Sarmizegetusa (Grădiştea Muncelului) or Racoş-Tipia Ormenişului[7] (Braşov county). As gold in all probability became a monopoly of the king, it disappeared almost completely from local sites only be found in great amounts in Sarmizegetusa, the capital of the Dacian state. Localized aristocrats were left to display only silver tableware and jewelry.

In the first quarter of the last century BC the Getae King Burebistas emerged as a strong authoritarian figure. During his long reign running from about

3   The theory is based on the discovery and research of several tomb association displaying different types of weapons and funerary practices. They were dated over the two centuries, earlier in the Balkans, later in Oltenia, Muntenia, southern Transylvania, the Mureş Valley and even further north, into historical Maramureş.

4   Cătălin Borangic, Marius Barbu - Caii şi cavaleri în spaţiul geto-dac. Istorie, pragmatism şi legenda, (unpublished)

5   Necropolis (from the Greek nekros, "death," and polis, "city"), a word used in arcaeological literature for pagan burial grounds. The ritual and type of burial had changed so that no archaeological traces were left.

6   Jordanes, the Roman historian of Gothic origin, wrote that Mars was worshiped by the Getae in a savage ritual (his victims were killed prisoners), considering that the God of War needed to be appeased with human blood. (Getica, 41)

7   On a dominant hill close to the river Olt Gorges, somewhere between Augustin and Racoş, archeologists discovered a hill with man-made terraces and a sacred area comparable with the one at Sarmizegetusa, but less conserved. The plateau near the top of the hill had six terraces supported by walls. Until the Roman conquest, seven temples – both circular and square – were in function there. (Researches coordinated by archaeologist Florea Costea from Braşov).

Dacian silver vessels from the Sâncrăieni Treasure (Harghita county), probably the most exquisite sample of Dacian art from the classical period (1ˢᵗ century BC - 1ˢᵗ century AD). Photo: George Nica, Radu Oltean © - MNIR București.

82 to 44 BC, he created a unified kingdom wielding important military power. How did Burebistas manage to bring together the ever conflicting tribes that Strabo had described as "reduced to an evil plight by numerous wars"? It was the same historian who implied that the King was helped by Decaeneus *("To help him secure the complete obedience of his tribe he had as his coadjutor Decaeneus, a wizard, a man who not only had wandered through Egypt, but also had thoroughly learned certain prognostics through which he would pretend to tell the divine will;* Geography, VII, 3, 11[8]*)* who was appointed viceroy and invested with enormous authority. "Within a short time he was set up as god," wrote Strabo. He may have been the one to unify the local religions, perhaps imposing his own cult to serve the royal authority and increase control over the tribal centers.

It thus appears that the king used religion and priests, akin to druids, to organize and discipline the warring tribes of Getae and Dacians. In Strabo's words: *"setting himself in authority over the tribe, restored the people, who had been reduced to an evil plight by numerous wars, and raised them to such a height through training, sobriety, and obedience to his commands that within only a few years he had established a great empire and subordinated to the Getae most of the neighboring peoples"* (Geography, VII, 3, 11).

---

8   English text by W. Falconer, M.A. The Perseus Digital Library.

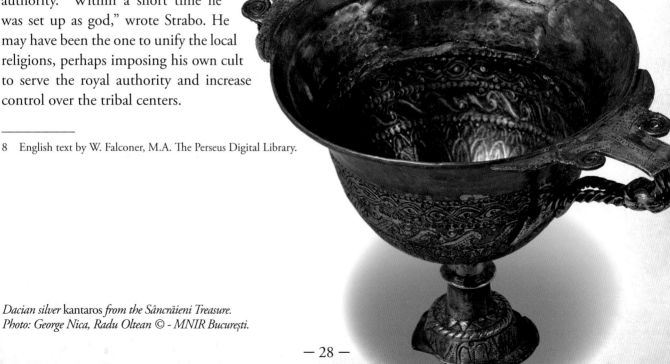

Dacian silver kantaros from the Sâncrăieni Treasure.
Photo: George Nica, Radu Oltean © - MNIR București.

Indeed, Burebistas attacked and conquered several Celtic tribes in western Transylvania and on the middle course of the Danube, probably defeating Bastarnae in northern Moldova and then focusing on the rich Greek merchant-cities on the Black Sea coastline.

These campaigns brought him in direct and long term contact with the Hellenistic civilization, which from then on spread fast into the territories north of the Carpathians. We don't know whether Burebistas ruled his huge kingdom from Sarmizegetusa. Probably not, since his connections and interests were in the Hellenistic south, on the Danube. After his death the kingdom was divided back again, into four and then five parts. But from then on, it was from the Orăştiei Mountain Range that Dacian kings and great priests emerged as political, military and religious rulers of the other areas.

Zalmoxis

The Dacian deity was known to ancient writers exclusively from the already popular writings of Herodotus, who depicted the Getae south of the Danube, those in contact with the Greeks, in the 5th century BC. All Greek and Roman authors who wrote about Zalmoxis over the following centuries had his *Histories* rather than their own experience, as a primary source. In time, Greek and Roman historians, fascinated by the exotic god, wrote about him without further research or any new information.

Zalmoxis had become a myth even in ancient times. He was worshiped as a God in the lower Danube River basin, where the Getae lived in the 6th and 5th centuries BC. Historians have shown that rituals used by Getae in Herodotus' time were completely different than those in Burebistas' time. Most researchers agree that his worship had ended in the classical Dacian period, 500 years after Herodotus.

Geto-Dacians? Or Getae and Dacians?

We should stop for a while to analyze the meaning of the terms Getae and Dacians, massively distorted by politics and ideology, especially during Nicolae Ceauşescu's Communist dictatorship from 1965 to 1989. The names were given by ancient writers of Greek or Latin background to the Thracian tribes living on both sides of the Lower Danube, from the Balkan Mountains to the Carpathians and beyond.

***Reconstruction of the Dacian Warrior** from Cugir. The cremation burial of an important Dacian leader, probably a king, was discovered in the 1980s near the Cugir fortification (town in Alba county), one of the oldest Dacian necropolises in Transylvania. The burial site was dated from the early 1st century BC, when Dacians consolidated their power in the Orăştiei Mountains.*

The deceased was laid on a four-wheeled funerary cart, next to which three horses were sacrificed. The inventory was extremely rich: silver fibulae (brooches); a gold decoration on the harness of one of the horses, most probably the riding steed; three bits; spurs; a long chain-mail coat with five gold plated silver buttons; a belt with a huge silver buckle; an iron helmet with face-guards in north-Italic tradition (unique in Transylvania); a long Celtic sword; a sica (dagger) with an iron scabbard; a shield; and a spear.

These authors, whose works covered over 700 years, were not seeking balance. Like today's journalists, some were better, others were less informed, some used generalization and clichés, others distorted reality for propaganda or political reasons. And more often than not, their works reached us incomplete, in fragments, or not at all. For these reasons ancient texts should be read prudently and critically.

We first learn about the Getae from Herodotus, known as the "Father of History", who placed them four centuries before the Dacians and in a completely different territory. He wrote in the 5th century BC about the Lower Danube Getae living south of the river, around Histria-Varna-Razgrad, areas close to the Black Sea better known to the Greeks.

Strabo, who lived from 63 BC to 19 AD, made a clear distinction between Dacians and Getae, although he mentioned that they spoke the same language. Ovid, the poet, also clearly described the Getae in Dobrogea "and their incomprehensible tongue", not the Dacians. It was only by the end of Burebistas' reign, in mid 1st century BC, that four decades of political, cultural and religious unification must have homogenized the two Northern Thracian peoples. The closer we get to Trajan's time, the less difference chroniclers made between the Danube Getae and the mountain Dacians, so that the two names tended to become synonymous.

Dacians make a late appearance on the historical stage. No one mentions them until the last century BC. They are first mentioned as such by Julius Caesar himself in his *De Bello Gallico*. It is clear that the name Dacians was connected to the inner Carpathian depression. We have already said that they were related to the warrior groups arriving in Transylvania from the south in the 2nd century BC. There, they mixed with the local population long dominated by the Celts.

By the next century, Transylvanian Dacians were apparently strong enough to get involved in one way or another in the Balkan strife. Large quantities of silver coins flowed north into Transylvania, probably as payment for military services at a moment of intense warfare in the Balkans. It was the time when the classical Dacian culture emerged and spread into the neighboring regions.

Until Burebistas' time, the history of Dacians north of the mountains had very little to do with that of the Danube Getae. Although Dacians were obviously related to the ancient Getae, it is a mistake to consider them one people before the last century BC. Though by

The chain-mail coat found in a cremation burial near the Getic dava at Popești, (village, Giurgiu county) dated 2nd – 1st century BC. It was discovered in one of the tumuli in the cemetery and belonged to a high-ranking warrior. The remains of military equipment were found next to a knife, fragments of a horse bit, a silver coin and pieces of ceramic. They included a decayed bronze helmet (later badly reconstructed), a bended Celtic sword, an arrow head, a curved dagger (sica) and a folded chain-mail coat. Photo: George Nica, Radu Oltean © - MNIR București.

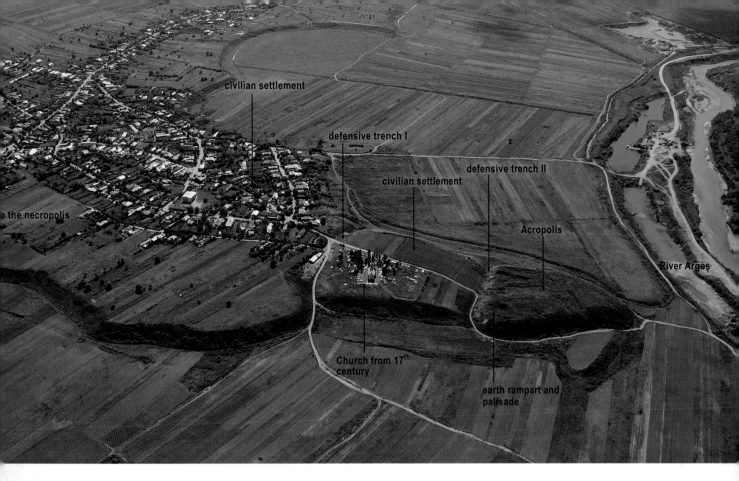

Aerial view of the Popeşti dava, an important Getic tribal center in the Wallachian plains, built on a natural terrace of the Argeş River. The settlement was targeted by the Roman expedition led by Sextus Aelius Catus (ca. 9-12 AD) and ceased to exist shortly after. Photo (2008): Carmen Bem.

the 1st century AD, Dacian and Getae were sometimes treated as one, sometimes correctly differentiated, but in general Greek authors preferred to name all northern Thracians as "Getae" while Latin ones named them "Dacians". The term Geto-Dacians is a modern compilation from the 1930s, but the term was glorified in the nationalistic Communist era when it became a dogma to be embraced by all historians and archaeologists.

This convention was useful to some extent and is now generally used to define certain common elements of the Getae and Dacian culture, such as their language, but only for the period between the 2nd century BC and 1st AD. The term is less relevant when it comes to ethnicity.

THE WARS WITH THE ROMANS

One-hundred-and-fifty years before Trajan the word Getae was, according to propaganda writings, synonymous with war, plunder and insecurity. Once Burebistas came to power, barbarians north of the Danube (Bastarnae, Dacians, Getae, Sarmatians, etc) became a force the Empire had to take into account.

After Burebistas' kingdom fell apart, Dacian and Getae leaders got involved in warfare against the Empire in the Balkans and their numerous plundering raids south of the Danube alarmed Augustus. Like Julius Caesar before him, the Emperor wanted to deal with the problem. But Rome did not plan to expand beyond the Danube, so conquest was not an option. Other solutions needed to be found.

Trajan's expeditions against Decebalus and the conquest of Dacia closed a long history of conflict between the Romans and Lower Danube tribes. It started long before when the frontiers of the Empire encroached on the Balkan Peninsula. This proximity was not always a source of conflict. It enhanced commercial relations as tradesmen found lucrative markets in the Getic and Dacian kingdoms.

Romans reach the Lower Danube

On the Black Sea shore, ancient Greek colonial cities thrived, spreading Hellenistic culture. Some of them – such as Histria, Tomis (Constanţa), Callatis (Mangalia), Odessos (Varna), Mesembria (Nesebar), Apollonia Pontica (Sozopol) – had been temporarily controlled by king Burebistas. Around 29 BC, Romans reached the Danube and started building a defense system, while the Greek port cities became Roman protectorates. The rest of the Thracian territory was under the control of

Dacian campaign against the Celts | Burebista
Caesar's first mention of Dacians
Romans on the Lower Danube - Licinius Crassus
Marcus Vinicius leads a campaign against the Getae
ca 9-12 – Campaign and dep of the Getae by Aelius Catus

BC - AD

80 70 60 50 40 30 20 10 5 5 10

R E P U B L I C
Civil war
Augustus

89-84 – The first Mithridatic War
73 – Slave uprising led by Spartacus
52 – Caesar defeats Vercingetorix at Alesia
44 – Caesar is assassinated
31– Battle of Actium

Chronology of events in this chapter

local leaders, sometimes aggressive, sometimes peaceful. They would soon react to the expanding Roman rule.

In 29-28 BC, we learn from historian Cassius Dio about a violent clash involving Roman general M. Licinius Crassus, three Getae kings controlling small territories in Scythia Minor (Dobrogea), Rholes, Dapyx and Zyraxes, and an army of Bastarnae (Germanic tribes living in southern and central Moldavia, neighbors and allies of the Getae). Rholes, a dynastic king in southern Dobrogea, was an ally of general M. Licinius Crassus in his attempt to liquidate the hostile centers of power led by Dapyx and Zyraxes. In one of the closing episodes of this conflict, we learn about a Getae fortress, Genucla (unknown location), besieged by the Roman troops and conquered following negotiations between Romans and a Greek-speaking Geta. To thank him for his help, Emperor Augustus personally named Rholes (whom he met in Corinth, Greece) a friend and ally of Rome.

Ovid, the poet, exiled by Rome to the Black Sea shore, often wrote about the unpredictable attacks of Getae warriors on Dobrogea cities like Aegissus (Tulcea) and Troesmis (Turcoaia, Tulcea county) and about the terror their riders and their poisonous arrows produced.

Starting in 11 BC and ending with the assassination

of the last Thracian king, Rhometalkes III, in 45 AD, the territories south of the Danube became client kingdoms and Rome sent in more and more troops to fortify the line of the river. After 46 AD, Thracia between the Balkans and the Danube was swallowed by the Empire as the Roman province of Moesia.

Back to Augustus' long reign, around 10-9 BC, we learn of a new Roman expedition against the Getae, led by Praetorian general Marcus Vinicius. This time, the Romans crossed the Danube into the enemy territory to confront the Getae on their own turf. Starting with this punishing expedition, Romans launched a long term policy of weakening the Getae and their allies. During the last decade of the 1st century BC, authors of the time mention campaigns against the Dacians and Sarmatians led by Cornelius Lentulus, probably a governor of Macedonia or one of the first imperial representatives in Moesia (northern Bulgaria nowadays). He led a campaign against the Getae north of the Danube. About the highlander Dacians, we learn from Latin historian Florus, who wrote:

"The Dacians cling close to the mountains, whence, whenever the Danube froze and bridged itself, under the command of their King Cotiso they used to make descents and ravage the neighboring districts. Though

Bronze oil lamp chandelier
with three arms, of Hellenistic provenience. It was found in the Getic dava at Piscul Crăsani (Ialomița county). The settlement was probably destroyed by Sextus Aelius Catus' expedition (ca 9-12 AD). An almost identical candlestick was discovered in 1949 at the Dacian site of Piatra Roșie (Luncani, Hunedoara county). Photo: George Nica, Radu Oltean © - MNIR București.

...yges settle in the Tisza Plains

...s exiled to Tomis
...created

46 – The whole Balkan region becomes a
Roman province -
Ripa Traciae and Moesia

Ca. 57- 67– Tiberius Plautius Silvanus Aelianus deports
100,000 people from the north to the south of the Danube

69 – Danube barbarians attack
Civil war in the Roman Empire

Diurapaneus

86 – Oppius Sabinus is killed in battle
87 – Cornelius Fuscus is killed in battle
88 – Tettius Iulianus defeats Decebalus at Tapae

Decebal

109 – Tropeum Traiani
113 – The column is inaugurated
106 – Dacia province established

| 30 | 40 | 50 | 60 | 70 | 80 | 90 | 100 | 110 | 120 |

Tiberius

Caligula

Claudius

Nero

**Galba
Otho
Vitellius**

79 – Vesuvius erupts

Vespasian

Titus

Domitian

Nerva

101-102 – First expedition
against Decebalus

Trajan

105-106 – Second expedition
against Decebalus

Hadrian
(117 - 138)

they were most difficult to approach, Caesar (Augustus) resolved to drive back this people. He, therefore, sent Lentulus and pushed them beyond the further bank of the river; and garrisons were posted on the nearer bank. On this occasion, then, Dacia was not subdued but its inhabitants were moved on and reserved for future conquest". (Florus, II, 29, English translation by E.S. Forster, Loeb Classical Library Edition, 1929)

S. Aelius Catus

An expedition led by proconsul Sextus Aelius Catus against the Getae in Wallachia, probably after 4 AD, had long term consequences. The vast majority of *davae* (towns, usually fortified) and settlements in the southern Romanian plains, all the way to the Carpathian Mountains foothills, disappeared around that time and a large number of locals (Strabo mentions around 50,000 Getae) were deported and resettled south of the Danube into Roman controlled lands. The Empire sought to reduce the military power of the Getae by de-populating an area that had proven dangerous for them and turning it into a safety zone for the Danube frontier. Archaeologists discovered that most *davae* were burned down and emptied at the beginning of the 1st century AD; some remained deserted, others resumed their lives at a much humbler level.

In another instance, mentioned by Suetonius, a Dacian army invaded imperial territory, but Dacians were forced to accept Roman authority after the troops killed three Dacian chieftains and many of their warriors. During Emperor Tiberius' reign, the Romans placed an extra buffer between themselves and the Dacians by bringing a Sarmatian population, the Iazyges, to colonize the area between the western Pannonia Province and Dacia between the Danube and the Tisza rivers.

Rome moved to consolidate the borders not just by forceful action, but also by diplomatic treaties (*foedera*) with barbarian kings all along the frontiers (*limes*). Romans were thus purchasing peace by trying to attract barbarian kings (Dacians, Getae, Bastarnae[9], Sarmatians[10]) into their system of client kingdoms and offering them major gains (*stipendia*) and political advantages - acknowledgement of their control over territories, their position, their authority in relation with neighbors (whether or not of the same people), the status of friends and allies of Rome, plus money and technical and military assistance. In exchange, the kings were supposed to act as allies, to protect the common frontiers from other invasions and, obviously, to refrain from any attack against Roman territories.

We do not know for sure when Dacians first became clients of Rome, probably as early as Augustus (27-14 AD). But the treaties were often broken by both Getae and Dacians – which made them known among their contemporaries as peoples who never acted in good faith (*"...Dacorum gens nunquam*

---

9   Germanic population living in north-eastern Dacia, between the Carpathians and the river Dniestr, between the 2nd century BC and the 1st century AD (the Poieneşti-Lukaševka culture).

10   The presence of the Sarmatians (whom the contemporaries named Sauromants), especially the tribes called Roxolani, in Moldavia and Muntenia, was stronger at the time than previously known. A people of nomad warriors of Iranian origin, related to the Scythians, they controlled the northern steppes by the Black Sea for a long time. Another Sarmatian people, the Iazyges, entered the regions between the Danube and the Tisza in the first century AD. They would become allies of the Romans in their wars against the Dacians.

Scythian-type, three-notched bronze arrow heads, with stub tangs, found at the Getic dava at Poiana (Galaţi county). About 4 cm long. Dated 2nd-1st century BC. Photo: George Nica, Radu Oltean © - MNIR Bucureşti.

fida...";Tacitus, *Hist.*, III, 46, 2). An explanation of Dacian attacking Romans in spite of the *foedera* could be that they tried to force the Romans to upgrade their payments. When payments stopped or emperors changed, Dacians would launch preventive attacks, to make sure they were not forgotten or to force new treaties with raised *stipendia*.

Later, in Nero's time, during an expedition across the river, Moesia's governor Tiberius Plautius Silvanus Aelianus forcefully moved 100,000 people south of the Danube (the Istrum, as it was named then). The Getae, Bastarnae, Sarmatians, with families, princes and kings, were sent to Moesia to work in order to pay tribute and take their minds off warfare and plundering – says a funerary eulogy for the governor, commonly known as the Tibur inscription. It's quite likely though that the migration was organized voluntarily, following an agreement between Romans and some barbarian kings seeking economic advantages and the safety of the Roman territory.

During the military anarchy that followed Nero's death (68-69 AD), when no less than three emperors succeeded in the year 69 AD alone, many troops were withdrawn from the Danube to support one or the other of the contenders, until Vespasian acceded to the throne. Taking advantage of the circumstances, groups of Dacians, Getae and Roxolan Sarmatians, crossed the river to attack the Roman territory. We don't know whether they were in breach of any treaties, but they could well have been, because the Romans, caught in civil strife, had failed to pay the *stipendia*. In the winter of 68-69, Roxolani crossed the Danube and massacred two Roman units and the following winter they attacked with 9,000 mounted men and plundered Moesia. They were defeated by Legion III Gallica led by Aponius Saturnius. Then the Dacians attacked:

"The Dacians, also, never trustworthy, became uneasy and now had no fear, for our army had been withdrawn from Moesia. They watched the first events without stirring; but when heard that Italy was aflame with war and that the whole empire was divided into hostile camps, they stormed the winter quarter of our auxiliary foot and horse and put themselves in possession of both banks of the Danube." (Tacitus - Histories III, 4 6; English translation by Clifford H. Moore, Loeb Classical Library, 1925)

During a new attack of the Roxolani in Moesia in the winter of 69-70 AD, they crossed the river when it froze solid. The Roman governor Fonteius Agrippa

was killed and two legions, I Italica and V Alaudae were defeated. After Vespasian came to power, Romans re-organized their army and further fortified the Danube banks, building camps and mobilizing new legions and auxiliaries to protect the frontiers. At the same time, they put together a strong Danube fleet: the Classis Flavia Moesica, based in Ratiaria and/ or Sexaginta Prista (see map). Ultimately peace along the frontiers of the Empire was yet again purchased by recognizing Dacia as Rome's client state.

DOMITIAN'S DACIAN WARS

During Domitian's rule, when the Emperor's boundless pride made him demand that he should be honored as a living god, the Empire had to face even more violent clashes with Lower Danube barbarians. Among them, the same "untamed" Dacians, Sarmatians, Marcomanni and others, as the chronicles of the time put it. This time, Dacian attacks signaled demands for further benefits from their relationship with Rome. If Dacian kings were already bound by treaties, their attacks probably meant that the *stipendia* had been reduced or paid with delays. Dacians crossed the frozen Danube and charged the winter camps of the Roman army, killing, looting and burning. It was the winter of 85 to 86 AD. These plundering raids appeared to be largely political in motivation.

Trying to stop the Dacian invasion, Moesia's Governor Oppius Sabinus lost his life in a fierce battle along with 3,000 of his legionaries. The fight probably took place near Adamclisi, in eastern Dobrogea, where a monumental complex - a mausoleum and an altar - would be erected before Trajan's time to honor a general and "the bravest of men who died for their homeland". It is possible, though, that Governor Oppius Sabinus was killed during another attack against the Legion headquarters at Novae.

In retaliation for this humiliating defeat, Domitian prepared a counteroffensive against Dacia. Starting with a reorganization of the Moesia province, he strategically divided it into two military-region sub-regions - Moesia Inferior and Superior. In 86, Domitian himself, accompanied by Praetorian Guard Prefect Cornelius Fuscus, marched to the Danube and, after hard battles, forced the Dacian armies back north across of the River and out of Roman controlled territory. The Dacian ruler in Sarmizegetusa at that time was probably Diurapaneus (Durpaneus), who in

short order either willingly or by force yielded power to Decebalus.

The new king, unwilling to fight the Romans, sent a peace envoy, but his message was contemptuously rejected by the Romans. Offended, Decebalus sent a second messenger, mockingly asking Domitian to buy peace from him by making every Roman citizen pay him two coins each year; if not they could expect war and great misery. In the spring of 87, angered by the ridicule and foregoing normal precautions, Cornelius Fuscus led a large army made up of Legion V Alaudae and many auxiliary units across the Danube on a floating bridge where the river narrows dramatically above the Iron Gates.

The details of what transpired are not clear as records describing the events were lost. What is known for sure is that Fuscus' army suffered a terrible defeat. His army was decimated and plundered by the Dacians to the extent that Legion V Alaudae practically ceased to exist. Fuscus was killed. The Legion V standards, weapons and war machines were taken as booty to be

One of the trophies on the Capitoline balustrade, in Rome, *mis-identified as the "Trophies of Marius". They probably date from Domitian's reign. One is dedicated to the war against the Germans and the other (reproduced here) to the Dacian Wars. After Domitian's death in 96, many of his monuments and inscriptions were destroyed as a result of the damnatio memoriae judgment, therefore we cannot be sure where the two trophies came from. Renaissance etchings show them decorating a monumental artesian fountain (nimpheum), the Castello dell'aqua Marcia. In 1590, by order of the Pope, they were taken and relocated to the Capitoline balustrade, where we may see them today. Weapons sculpted on the trophy are mostly Roman, but the heavily decorated shields may be barbarian. Note the four arrow bags and the bows decorated with wolf heads.*

*The same monument reconstructed in **Pietro Santi Bartoldi**'s album **Colonna Traiana**, late 17th century. Even then, the trophy was thought to be connected to Trajan's reign and the Dacian Wars. BAR.*

recovered fifteen years later, in 102, when Emperor Trajan's troops found them in a Dacian fortress.

Dacians were defeated at *Tapae*...

Rome renewed its attacks a year later when General Tettius Iulianus, a prudent man with considerable experience fighting Lower Danube tribes, was sent in to continue the war. In 68-69, he had battled the Dacians and Sarmatians. This time, Romans mobilized massive forces and at least four Legions (III Scythica, V Macedonica, II Adiutrix, VII Claudia).

Again crossing the Danube on pontoon bridges, the invading army marched from the western Banat region towards the Carpathian Mountains and the Dacian capital. A decisive battle took place at *Tapae*, identified by historians as a mountain pass also known as The Iron Gate of Transylvania. All these details were recounted in Cassius Dio's writings (67,

10, 1-3). Fighting was fierce with countless Dacians killed. Vezina (Avezina),[11] one of Decebalus' chief aides, survived by hiding among the dead waiting for the dark to make his escape.

The Tapae victory erased the shame brought by the defeat of Oppius Sabinus and Cornelius Fuscus. But the advantage gained quickly dissipated. Facing unexpected and serious threats in Germania where a menacing uprising had started led by Antonius Saturninus, Governor of Germania Superior, Domitian ordered a rapid withdrawal cutting short the Dacian campaign.

In tandem, the Emperor set out to punish Germanic tribes in Pannonia – Marcomanni, Quadi and Sarmatian Iazyges – for refusing to support the Romans against the Dacians and thus indirectly supporting the latter. According to historian Cassius Dio[12] undertaking ended in complete disaster and much to Dacia's unexpected benefit.

"Domitian, having been defeated by Marcomani, took to flight, and hastily sending messages to Decebalus, king of the Dacians, induced him to make a truce, though he himself had hitherto refused to grant one in response to the frequent requests of Decebalus. And so Decebalus accepted his overtures, for he had suffered grievous hardships; yet he did not wish to hold a conference with Domitian personally, but instead sent Diegis, (his brother) with the men, to give him the arms and a few captives, who, he pretended, were the only ones he had".

... but Decebalus won the war

In Rome, Decebalus' brother Diegis went before the Senate and symbolically deposed the weapons. In an impressive ceremony, Domitian himself placed a gold diadem on the envoy's head thus making the visit of the Dacians to Rome was a great success.

We learn from Cassius Dio that *"the truce had cost (Domitian) something besides his losses, for he had given large sums of money to Decebalus on the spot, as well as artisans of every trade pertaining to both peace and war, and had promised to keep on giving large sums in the future".* (67, 7, 4, English translation by Earnest Cary, Loeb Classical Library, Harvard University Press 1914-1927)

Emperor Domitian in armor. Heavily restored marble statue from the collection of the Vatican Museum, Rome.

11   According to historian Dan Dana, the real name of Decebalus' chief councilor was Avezina, a name often found in the Thracian and Dacian onomastics. The form Vezina could have been an error of the mediaeval copyist.

12   Cassius Dio (2nd century AD) wrote Historia Romana, a history of Rome in the Greek language, in 80 volumes. The books describing the Dacian wars reached us in the form of excerpts copied by byzantine monks Ioannes Xiphilinos of Constantinople (11th century) and Zonaras (12th century).

But Decebalus would have to become an ally and friend of Rome, allowing Roman troops to cross his territory as often as required by the situation to grant peace alongside the Danube – this endless frontier of the Empire. The territory between the Carpathians and the Danube remained under the attentive control of the Romans, with at least 2-3 fortified bridgeheads installed on the Dacian bank.

In Rome, Domitian like a true victor celebrated his triumph against the Dacians. But Cassius Dio was more critical in his own observations.

"He graced the festival that followed with many exhibits appropriate to a triumph, though they came from no booty that he had captured; (…) The exhibits which he displayed really came from the store of imperial furniture". (ibid. (67, 7, 4).

Following what had been a bloody and wearisome war, peace seemed to please everyone. Domitian aimed not at an annexation of Dacia, but at the pacification of the region and reinforcement of the Danube frontier. The Senate even wanted to reward the Emperor with the name of Dacicus (conqueror of Dacians), but he refused and only kept the name Germanicus.

Decebalus was also pleased that his new status as an ally of the Empire and friend and partner of the Roman people (*rex sociusque et amicus*) brought him supplementary income, qualified engineers, power and authority in relation with potential local enemies, chiefly the Sarmatian Iazyges to the northeast.

But then came a new crisis. In September 96 AD, Domitian was assassinated. This ended the short-lived Flavian dynasty, which included Vespasian and his two sons, Titus and Domitian. The first two were remembered as good Emperors while Domitian hardly so. The Roman Senate in a severe rebuque applied the sanction *damnatio memoriae*, a condemnation after death, a stigma applied to emperors or noblemen who seriously betrayed and discredited the Roman state.

Following that sanction, the immediate followers to the throne, Nerva and Trajan, tried to erase any trace of Domitian and any memory of his successes. Ancient authors, influenced by the decision of the Senate to damn the emperor's memory did not describe his fight against the Dacians in an objective way, preferring to insist on defeats and minimizing his victories. The way we understand the Dacian wars is influenced both by the loss of written documents and by the subjective sources of the time, hostile to Domitian and favoring Trajan. That is why Trajan's wars in Dacia are better understood when seen through the lens of Domitian's legacy. The two years separating Domitian's reign from that of Trajan were a mere respite, caused by Emperor Nerva's incapacity to continue what his predecessor had started.

Modern history has partially rehabilitated Domitian's reign. His abuses only affected the elites including members of the Senate (and they, of course, are the ones writing history), but his governing was well organized and problems were wisely solved, bringing prosperity to the Empire.

A SHORT HISTORY OF RESEARCH IN THE ORĂŞTIEI MOUNTAINS

Ever since the 16th century, the ruins and treasures found in the Orăştiei/Şureanu Mountains have captured the imagination of locals, travelers and of treasure hunters alike. A Dacian treasure found by peasants on the banks of the Strei River around 1540 ended up in the hands of Gheorghe Martinuzzi, Archbishop of Esztergom and Governor of the Transylvanian Principality. The first notes about a Dacian citadel surface early in the 19th century. The Austrian fiscal agent for Hunedoara county, Pál Török, reported to Vienna in 1803 about extraordinary treasures found by farmers among the ruins of an ancient "city" in Grădiştea Forest, believed to be a Roman construction. After digs carried out under orders of the imperial Treasury, Török wrote a long report on the nature of the local ruins, a key document for understanding the archaeological realities of the time.

In 1805, a military engineer and architect, Major Mihály Péchy, published a new report, describing the remains of the Great Circular Sanctuary for the first time and referencing the Roman thermal baths ruins. In 1838, pastor Johann Michael Ackner, a passionate amateur archaeologist declared that the Grădiştea Muncelului ruins were surely not Roman. He argued that Romans would never have chosen such unfriendly locations to start colonies. In 1844, András Fodor, chief doctor of Hunedoara county, conducted a small scale dig at the Roman baths

site, publishing a summary of his findings. Around 1900, archaeologist Gábor Téglás considered that the citadel on Grădiştea Hill was Decebalus' last refuge, protected by the fortifications at Cugir, Piatra Roşie, Ponorici and Costeşti. Professor Gábor Finály reported in 1910, after field research in the area, that the Orăştiei Mountains ruins were not Roman but Dacian citadels destroyed by Trajan. They belonged, he concluded, to a culture unknown so far. At the proposal of a committee that included the professor, the Austro-Hungarian Ministry of Agriculture declared Grădiştea Muncelului - over 591 *arpents* (some 250 hectares) of secular forest – as a natural monument.

Prior to WWI, the Society for History, Archaeology and Natural Sciences of Hunedoara County forwarded a memoir to the General Inspectorate of Museums and Libraries, suggesting that Dacian and Roman ruins in the Grădiştea Muncelului area and other historical sites be explored and uncovered.

At the advice of Vasile Pârvan and with the financial support of the Historical Monuments Commission, professor D. M. Teodorescu (1881–1947) from Cluj University aided by Al. Ferenczi (1894–1945) conducted systematic digs at the Orăştiei Mountains from 1924 to 1929.

In 1943 during WW-II, Constantin Daicoviciu (1889–1973) continued to dig at Costeşti. In 1949, he started a single dig at Piatra Roşie (Luncani

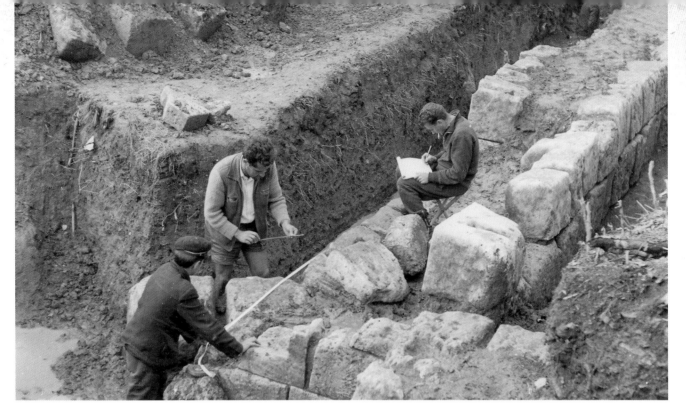

Historical photographs taken during the archaeological digs at the Dacian citadels (the Daicoviciu Archive).
Left: Constantin Daicoviciu in 1944, in front of the monumental stairway at Costeşti.
Above: Hadrian Daicoviciu and Ioan Glodariu at Feţele Albe in 1966. © MNIT - Cluj-Napoca.

Perspective view over the Orăştiei /Şureanu Mountains, indicating civilian settlements, citadels and other Dacian fortifications, researched or merely located.

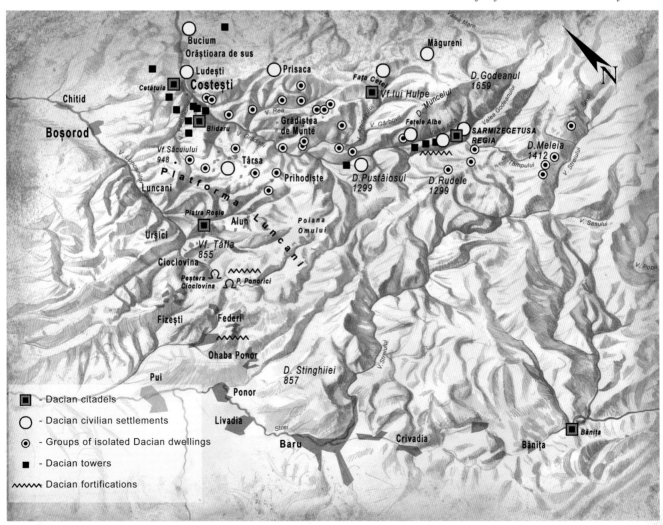

- **■** - Dacian citadels
- **○** - Dacian civilian settlements
- **◉** - Groups of isolated Dacian dwellings
- **■** - Dacian towers
- **⌁** Dacian fortifications

village), followed by publication of a monograph. In 1950, the team led by C. Daicoviciu started to uncover Sarmizegetusa's ruins at a rapid pace. Hundreds of cubic meters of earth were moved with mine-carts and many archaeologically details, including Roman culture layers, were only recorded superficially, if at all. A few years later, the Sacred Area and Roman fort were uncovered and the dwellings on several terraces dug out. Surprisingly their locations were not marked on a general map of the site. Compared to subsequent years, we may say that the 1950s were rich in elaborately illustrated publications with drawings and photos. But stratigraphic sections were then very rare and a lot of other information was left out unmentioned and unrecorded, therefore lost forever.

The Blidaru citadel was unearthed and research continued at Costești. Digs at Căpâlna citadel lasted between 1942 and 1954 under the supervision of Mihail Macrea (1908–1967) and Dumitru Berciu (1907–1998), and were resumed later by Hadrian Daicoviciu and Ioan Glodariu. After C. Daicoviciu's death, researchers from Cluj who conducted the digs on the Orăștiei Mountains were coordinated by his son, Hadrian Daicoviciu (1932–1984). In the 70s, the walled settlement at Șesul cu Brânză was found on the Fețele Albe Hill. One of the participants at the Orăștiei/Șureanu[1] mountains digs was Ion Horațiu Crișan (1928–1994), the first archaeologist to suggest that the Dacian citadel of Sarmizegetusa surrounded the Sacred Area. He and Florin Medeleț (1943–2005) discovered a rich incineration tomb of a chief Dacian warrior during their digs at the Cugir necropolis. Unfortunately, their findings were never published.

Articles and archaeological field reports were less frequent and less consistent after the mid 70s. In the 1980s, when the communist state celebrated

with pomp 2050 years from "the first centralized and independent Dacian state led by Burebistas," a rapid restoration of the Sacred Area began. Nicolae Ceaușescu was expected to visit the archaeological site at Sarmizegetusa. To please him, concrete walls were poured to support the terraces – still not completely hidden from view today – and several limestone bases heavily eroded by time were replaced by "beautiful" cement copies. Other concrete cylinders were stored amidst the ruins – it was planned to replace all the originals – where they remained until 2010. Ceaușescu never arrived and the restoration was never completed because the funding was cut.

After Hadrian Daicoviciu's premature death, the team was led by Ioan Glodariu, who directly or indirectly coordinated all the archaeological digs along the Grădiștea Valley and in other sites in the Orăștiei Mountains. István Ferenczi, Eugen Iaroslavschi and Adriana Pescaru were also part of his research team. Lack of funding kept research at a modest level all through the 80s, but in 1989 a popular book was published synthesizing all the information related to the Dacian citadels in south-western Transylvania. Currently, Orăștiei Mountains research led by professor Gelu Florea of Babeș-Bolyai University is conducted in cooperation with archaeologists from the Transylvanian History Museum in Cluj and the Dacian and Roman Civilization Museum in Deva. Many other scholars and archaeologists who are not mentioned here worked hard to elucidate the history of these citadels.

ORĂȘTIEI MOUNTAINS IN DECEBALUS' TIME

Just before Trajan's wars, the mountain area around the Dacian capital was densely populated, much more so than today. Archaeologists found many signs that the place was inhabited 2,000 years ago - mountain villages, both spread on deforested hilltops and grouped together on man-made dwelling terraces. On alpine meadows, circular buildings were identified, perhaps the most efficient shape when facing mountain winds, with archeological evidence that made scientists believe they were either sheep pegs, or sanctuaries, or abodes of Dacian hermits or, most probably, given the

---

1 In this book, the mountains where most Dacian citadels are located have been named Orăștiei Mountains. In reality, they are a subdivision of the Șureanu or Șurianu Mountains, having the Parâng Mountains on the South, the Cindrel Mountains on the east and the Lotru mountains on the south-east. Hațeg Country and the Strei-Jiu corridor lay on the west and south-west. The river that cuts the Grădiștea Valley and runs into the Mureș near the city of Orăștie has two different names: upstream of Costești, in the mountainous region, it is named Grădiștea, while downstream it is known as the City River or Orăștiei. In the older archeological literature, one book uses both names without any specifications, creating confusion. This book only uses the name of Grădiștea River. The hill where Sarmizegetusa Regia is located is mentioned as Grădiștea Hill, Grădiștea Muncelului or Piciorul Muncelului.

large quantity of red clay found dwellings for seasonal workers extracting and crafting iron. Although the terrain was good for agriculture, its prosperity came from metal works (see chapter on iron) and from salt deposits – an important resource at the time, especially since it was scarce in the Balkans and Pannonia – as well as from the gold washed by mountain streams. The larger area around the capital also made use of the fertile valley of the Mureş River.

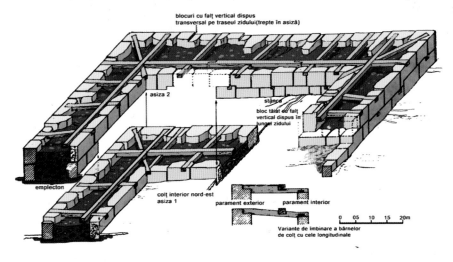

Căpâlna Citadel. An instance of murus dacicus. Axonometric reconstruction of the first rows of stone blocks and of the distribution of wooden beams in the foundation of the residential tower. Reconstruction was made possible by traces of charred wood found in the digs. After a drawing by architect Anişoara Sion, published in the monograph of Căpâlna (1989) by Ioan Glodariu and Vasile Moga.

Murus dacicus is the name given by archaeologists to the type of Hellenistic masonry used in some of the Dacian fortresses. In fact, it is a variety of the Greek wall named by the Romans *opus quadratum* and may be seen exclusively in a few citadels in the Orăştiei Mountains (plus the Piatra Craivii fortress, north of the Mureş River). This type of wall, widely used in the Greek world, consisted of two parallel rows of finely finished rectangular blocks. The blocks were fit tightly together because Dacians and Greeks did not use mortar. The wide space between the two rows was filled with earth and broken stone. To prevent the filling (*emplecton*) from pushing the walls apart, the two outer faces were bound by a lacing of wooden beams introduced in sparrow-tail shaped orifices.

The presence of Greek workers and master craftsmen from the Hellenistic world in Dacia is well established. Other elements or constructive solutions of Hellenistic tradition could be found in the Dacian sites, such as large bricks used in tower-houses or ceramic tiles and tubes.

These citadels bore little resemblance to the mediaeval fortifications we usually have in mind when we mention a "fortress". They were not built to withstand an organized siege. This danger did not exist when they were erected. They were primarily residential sites for the military and religious elite, including the king, well connected to the realities and fineries of the Greek, and lately Roman culture. Some historians claim that the network of citadels was devised as a unitary strategic complex meant to protect the capital. But the fortifications were erected independently and in distinct historical periods, over more than a

century. Of course, their defensive role must have been taken into consideration, but it's more likely that the aristocracy simply wanted to gravitate around the royal and religious centre at Sarmizegetusa.

Attempts to reconstruct them visually in this book are purely hypothetical, because definitive archaeological information is meager. We do not know what shape or height the towers were, whether the stone walls went all the way up to the roof-line or had intermediary stories built of wood, how the battlements on top of the walls looked, whether the wall-walk was covered or not, or how wide were the openings in the towers.

Reconstruction of the Costeşti Citadel before confrontations with the Romans
1. *Dwelling tower I;* **2.** *Dwelling tower II with monumental stair;* **3.** *Watch tower based on stone foundations (only 4 of 6 visible today);* **4.** *Traces of barracks, hearths and an oven;* **5.** *Temple, the only one in the main enclosure, dismantled during or before the Roman wars;* **6.** *The Great Temple outside the main enclosure;* **7.** *Gate in the stone wall;* **8.** *Part of the wooden rampart named by archaeologists "the red wall" because it burned into red clay during the clashes with the Romans (it was built on top of an older wall);* **9.** *Small stone towers overseeing the road to the citadel;* **10.** *Old wall;* **11.** *Cistern;* **12.** *Barracks of unidentified shape and size;* **13.** *Small temples;* **14.** *Isolated tower with wooden upper level;* **15.** *Traces of older palisades that used to protect the upper plateau;* **16.** *Tumulus mound for a 1st century AD warrior found in 1997 and incompletely documented (unpublished); Possibly larger necropolis.*

COSTEŞTI

The fortification on top of Cetăţuia (Little Fortress) Hill in Costeşti, whose Dacian name was lost in time, was built in a key strategic location, where the valley of the Grădiştea narrows down into the mountains.

Apparently, the Costeşti citadel is the oldest in the area, functioning as an important local political and religious center. It served as an acropolis to the settlement at the foot of the hill and alongside the river. The citadel was fortified in what historians defined as three separate stages. In the first phase, two tower dwellings were

erected on the hilltop plateau, in the most typical Hellenistic style, most certainly by craftsmen from the Black Sea ports. Monumental stone stairs led to the western tower. In the second phase, larger towers were built on the foundations of the old ones, using both stone and large, slightly burned bricks. The roofs were covered in typical Greek tiles and all details indicated that stonecutters and masons trained in Hellenistic techniques kept permanent workshops in the area.

Between the two hilltop palace-towers, traces of wooden buildings were found, including hearths and a bread oven. The stone foundations (six of them

Costești Citadel

Left: *Foundations of the wooden columns of a rectangular open temple. The stone bases were partially buried under the floor level. At some point during the wars against the Romans, foundations from one of the temples (probably already destroyed) were used to block the entrance in the stone wall.*

Above: *Stone foundations heaped into the gap in the wall (no. 7 on the illustrations above).*

Bottom: *Panoramic view on dwelling tower II and of the monumental stairway leading to it. At some point, there were rails along the stairway and it was covered by a roof supported by wooden pillars.*

initially, today only four left) holding the wooden pillars of an observation tower were also discovered here. The observation post would have been extremely useful, due to the excellent location providing visibility all the way to the Mureș Valley.

Three wood and earth ramparts were built over time on the hill sides. At some point, they were reinforced with four stone towers placed in the most exposed areas. Three of these towers were then linked by a massive wall with an artillery platform from which *ballistae* could be used defensively.

Three other isolated towers were built on terraces around the citadel. The largest of them was permanently occupied by a small garrison. Other artificial terraces under the hilltop plateau hosted the remnants of four temples – parallel rows of limestone that used to be foundations for wooden pillars.

After the first confrontations with the Romans, probably under Domitian, the old wood and earth rampart which surrounded the hilltop was replaced by a stronger and a more complex wooden structure, partly following the same line. One of the temples was then removed and the stone foundations of its pillars were used to block the gate in the stone wall. The new rampart was exposed to intense fire during the battles

Costești Citadel. *Detail of a Hellenistic wall. The foundation of the palace tower (no. II). The upper part of the tower was built using mud-brick – also a Greek influence.*

with the Romans and the color of the burned clay determined archaeologists to name it the Red Wall.

During Trajan's wars, Romans invested extensively in preparation of the siege of the Costești citadel. The traces of a small Roman camp (a *castellum)* were found on a low terrace at the foot of the hill - probably the base from where the attacks were launched. This is a proof that the fortress was not easy target and that its siege was difficult.

Blidaru Fortress in a hypothetical reconstruction, shortly before the war against the Romans. *In the background, the Grădiştea River valley.*
Legend: 1. *Initial enclosure;* ***2.*** *Second enclosure;* ***3.*** *Dwelling tower;* ***4.*** *Gate tower of the first enclosure;* ***5.*** *Gate tower of the second enclosure;* ***6.*** *Dismantled wall;* ***7.*** *Cistern;* ***8.*** *One of the isolated towers surrounding the fortress (the one in Poiana Perţii).*

Aerial view of the Blidaru Fortress ruins. *Photo: Dan Dimăncescu.*

Blidaru Fortress. *Ruins of the western tower of the second enclosure (the closest to the cistern). The edifice is not as carefully constructed as the rest of the citadel, suggesting that it was either built later, without qualified craftsmen, or put together in a hurry, during the war.*

Bottom-right: *A carefully built portion of wall in Blidaru's second enclosure.*

BLIDARU

Adjacent to the Dacian settlement found in the village of Costeşti, impressive ruins of the Blidaru fortress were unearthed on the ridge of a steep hill. A tower-shaped dwelling for the master or commander of the citadel stood in the middle of an irregular four-sided enclosure with corner towers. The entrance, through a gate in the small tower, would have forced the enemy, if they managed to enter the fortress, to turn sharply and expose their flank. Later on, an extra enclosure was added. The western wall of the first enclosure was torn down in order to unify the two courts. Food-storage vessels were found buried in a row of rooms built alongside two of the newly added walls. These rooms, probably some sort of barracks, were built in a simpler technique than *murus dacicus*, from roughly cut pieces of local stone alternating with finely cut limestone.

A new entrance was also built, not far from the old one. During the Roman wars, the old entrance was filled up with stone. A huge cistern was discovered a few meters away from the westernmost tower, outside the citadel. It is an 8/6/4 meter volume with a vaulted ceiling. And, unprecedently with the Dacians, it was built with stone and a special waterproof mortar containing coal dust. The masonry was then lined with layers of special

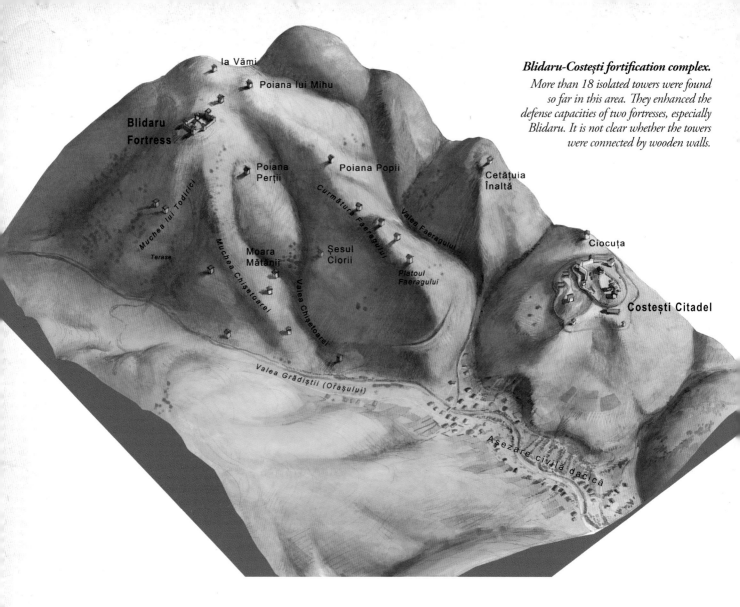

la Vămi

Poiana lui Mihu

Blidaru
Fortress

Poiana
Perţii

Poiana Popii

Muchea lui Todirici

Curmătura Faeragului

Cetăţuia
Înaltă

Terase

Muchea Chişeloarei

Moara
Mătănii

Şesul
Ciorii

Valea Chişeloarei

Valea Faeragului

Platoul
Faeragului

Ciocuţa

Costeşti Citadel

Valea Grădiştii (Oraşului)

Aşezare civilă dacică

Blidaru-Costeşti fortification complex.
*More than 18 isolated towers were found
so far in this area. They enhanced the
defense capacities of two fortresses, especially
Blidaru. It is not clear whether the towers
were connected by wooden walls.*

coating, meant to make it even more waterproof. It could hold over 190,000 liters (50,000 gallons) of water.

The technique indicates the presence of highly qualified masons from the Roman Empire, probably sent in as part of the treaty signed by Domitian and Decebalus. The water in the cistern was coming from at least one remote spring, as suggested by the fragments of ceramic tubes found in several locations. Traces of a temple (or probably two) with limestone foundations, almost entirely destroyed, were discovered by archaeologists on a plateau named Pietroasele lui Solomon, a few hundred meters from the village, on the way to Târsa. Another temple is expected to be found closer to the fortifications.

Close to Blidaru and in direct connection with the citadel, Dacians erected a system of eighteen or more isolated towers of finely cut blocks of stone and

the same type of foundations as the rest. The upper part of the towers was made of either plastered wood, burnt bricks, or *murus dacicus*. Bits of Greek ceramic tiles were found among the ruins. The towers and Blidaru were meant to create a fortification system not fully understood to this day. Towers might have been connected by palisades which either disappeared without a trace or are still to be discovered.

Recently unearthed foundations of one of the 2 isolated towers located in La Vămi (Poiana lui Mihu), about 500 meters (1,500 feet) from Blidaru fortress.

A possible reconstruction of the Piatra Roșie citadel. *The shape and number of civilian dwellings are hypothetical, because the area was not investigated. Terraces indicate that Dacians built here.*

PIATRA ROȘIE

Dacians carved a horizontal platform 160 meters long and at most 50 meters wide (500 and 160 feet respectively) on the top of a conical hill, isolated by vertical limestone ravines red with iron oxides. In the summer of 1949, Constantin Daicoviciu organized an archaeological campaign during which the remains of the citadel and of other buildings erected by the Dacians were uncovered. The citadel - with walls of soft, cleanly cut limestone erected in the same *murus dacicus* technique - covered two thirds of the artificial plateau. Towers were found on three of the corners, while a fourth can only be imagined, because the corner has long disappeared into the ravine. However, that fourth tower might not have been needed at all, since the steep rocks provided perfect protection. A monumental stairway led to the entrance, cut through the biggest tower. The stone slabs used for

the steps were unfortunately taken away by locals during the last 50 years. A fifth tower stood in the middle of the wall overseeing the access. The stone foundations of an unusual 40 meters (130 feet) long apsidal building were found inside the enclosure.

Two long wooden buildings on stone foundations once stood on the upper platform, outside the enclosure. Several round-shaped stone bases found next to them suggested that a temple had been dismantled by Dacians themselves.

A narrow path with a gentle slope led to the citadel, passing by man-carved terraces. The terraces have not been studied by archaeologists, but are believed to have supported houses or other buildings. The road to the tower gate was paved with wide slabs of stone fitted on top of each other like wide and very low stair-steps. Just outside the gate, a secondary path emerged from the main road and led to an apsidal building (the wall

opposite the entrance was shaped like a half cylinder). It is believed to have served as a worship place. In 1948, on one side of this building, Daicoviciu uncovered two iron discs that he believed to be parade shields.

The small sanctuary was erected above a huge doline, a natural funnel-shaped depression, typical for limestone regions. On the bottom of the funnel, archaeologists found several valuable artifacts, including a Celtic long sword. The doline could have been a place of worship its base perhaps sealed with clay, thus turning it into a sort of sacred lake where offerings were thrown. This is a merely speculative explanation to why several objects were found on its bottom and also why the apsidal building was built right over it.

The whole terraced area was once surrounded by a wall of wood, stone and earth. Remains of a mortared stone wall were found close to the place where the access way cut through the primitive wall. There is spirited debate among archaeologists regarding this

Piatra Roşie. *The limestone blocks paving the road preserved next to the hilltop doline.*

Eastward panorama from the village of Ursici towards the Piatra Roșie citadel (on the right) and the Luncani Plateau.
Numerous traces of Dacian houses were found on the Plateau, in the village of Târsa.

stretch of wall. Some argue that it or indeed, the whole wall is a late construction of the 12th-13th centuries. Their arguments are based on finding medieval ceramics and traces of lime mortar.[1] However, next to the lowest terraces, at the foot of the hill, four towers were unearthed. They had stone foundations and walls of large Hellenistic bricks, just like the towers in Costești, as well as ceramic tile roofs. Regrettably the Piatra Roșie citadel was never restored or placed under conservation. Many of the findings described above were lost to the elements or to locals and looters. The most serious loss is the monumental stairway of which not even one slab remains.

A block of soft, porous limestone, quarried in Măgura Călanului, coming from the wall of the Piatra Roșie citadel. The orifice in the upper side held one of the beams that held the wall together.

---

1   A type of mortar (quicklime with sand) that Dacians never used in their buildings, except for the special plasters used at the Blidaru cistern, a construction of the late period made with Roman assistance.

Piatra Roşie Hill. View from the north-east, from the outskirts of Târsa village. Note the hilltop plateau leveled by the Dacians.

BĂNIŢA

The fortress of Băniţa (Cetatea Bolii) was erected on a dramatically steeply rounded limestone outcrop, separated by water from the surrounding hills. Its walls were almost vertical and only one side was accessible, on a precipitous path. The traces of an ancient Dacian village at the bottom of the limestone mount were completely erased by the construction of a railroad. Access to the top was guarded by a 115 meter (375 foot) long wall pierced by a monumental stairway. Its limestone slabs are now almost entirely destroyed by the weather, because the ruins were in no way conserved after the archeological research.

The long, narrow plateau on top of the hill was divided into three terraces, bearing traces of *murus dacicus* as well as of mediaeval walls – a sign that the strategic location was still attractive in the Middle Ages. One of the Roman armies coming down on Sarmizegetusa began its ascent from the vicinity of this citadel. Archaeological evidence shows that the citadel was destroyed during the Roman wars and never rebuilt again.

Băniţa (Bolii) Hill.
View from the east.
Photo: Dan Oltean.

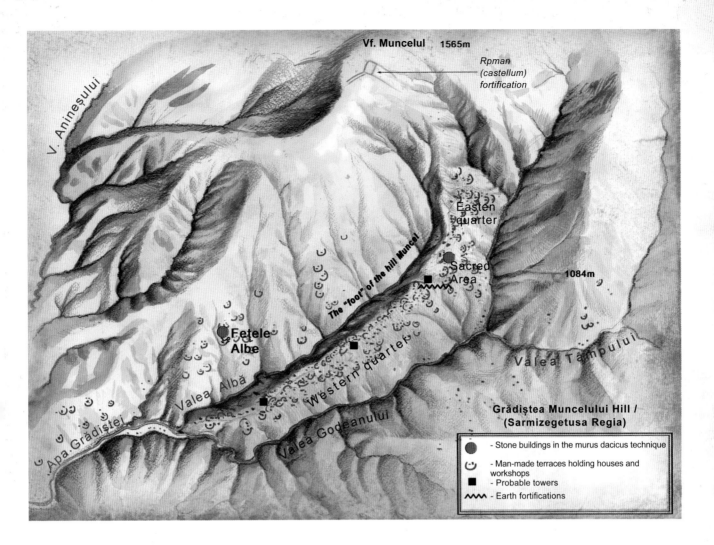

Map labels:
- Vf. Muncelul 1565m
- Rpman (castellum) fortification
- V. Aninesului
- V. Aninesului
- Easten quarter
- The "foot" of the hill Muncel
- Sacred Area
- 1084m
- Fetele Albe
- Western quarter
- Valea Tâmpului
- Valea Albă
- Valea Godeanului
- Apa Grădiștei
- Grădiștea Muncelului Hill / (Sarmizegetusa Regia)
- ◕ - Stone buildings in the murus dacicus technique
- ʊ - Man-made terraces holding houses and workshops
- ■ - Probable towers
- ᴧᴧᴧ - Earth fortifications

SARMIZEGETUSA REGIA

The most famed and largest Dacian settlement in the Orăştiei Mountains is by far the most isolated and hard to reach. On Grădiştea Muncelului at 1,000 meters high (3,200 feet), cold and wet for the most part of the year and lacking in resources, the semi-urban Dacian settlement was built along a narrow ridgeline squeezed between two deep valleys. Archaeologists refer to it as "Piciorul" Muncelului (the "Foot" of the Muncel) because the highest mountain in the area, the Muncel, seems to be resting on the Grădiştea Hill. The very word *grădişte* means small citadel in Slavic, a language introduced to the area a many centuries latter, indicating that the ancient fortifications were known to the locals.

Over 200 terraces were carved into the southern, sunnier side of the hill, holding houses, workshops and other buildings, most of them facing the road. The ancient road, paved with broken local stone, followed the ridge from the confluence of the two rivers below to the top of the Muncel.

Cutting all these horizontal platforms must have required a tremendous effort, probably lasting over 150 years or more. All dwellings and workshops were built in wood, but had stone foundations. The most important monuments, that made the fame of the place, stood midway from the foot of the hill and the top, in an agglomeration called "the Sacred Area". Monumental wood and stone temples were supported by massive limestone walls quarried 50 kilometers (30 miles) away. A limestone paved road led to the area. The temples were probably protected by an enclosure with strong walls and towers. The shape and size of the sacred citadel is practically unknown, because the area has been too little studied by archaeologists. Seriously damaged during the Roman wars, its stone slabs were dismantled for reuse in constructing a Roman fort nearby. Fortifications, once believed to be the real Sarmizegetusa, are recognized today to be a Roman construction, a camp adapted to field conditions in Dacia (see p.136).

Researchers consider the settlement on top of Grădiştea Muncelului to be a proto-urban development, almost a city. It was identified as Sarmizegetusa Regia, the political and religious capital of the Dacian Kingdom. The fact that the Romans considered it as important as to place a strong garrison next to it, first in a wood and earth camp and then in a stone

Reconstruction of the central area of Sarmizegetusa Regia.
1. The sacred enclosure and probably the greater Sarmizegetusa citadel (undiscovered yet);
2. Location of a possible Dacian fort (see the debate on Roman intervention, see p. 136);
3. Earth fortification, initially identified as Dacian, but most probably Roman, part of a camp built after 102 AD;
4. "La Tău"- A water source and swamp, one of the main supplies for the western quarter;
5. The six-terrace plateau researched in the 1950s. Its location is relative, because the general plan of the hill with researched areas has not been published to this day; **6.** The western quarter; **7.** The eastern quarter.

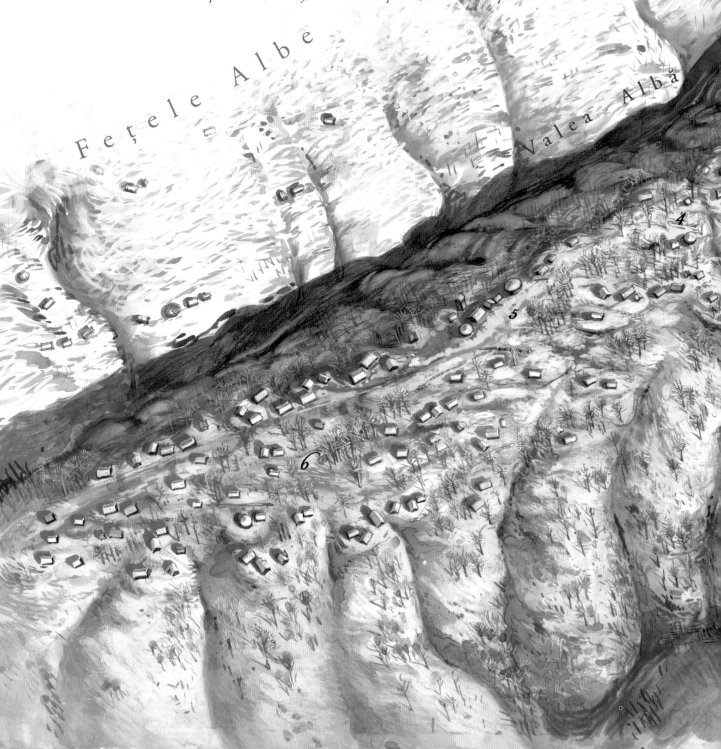

fortification, indicates once again that this must have been the ancient royal capital.

Scholars believe that the place started to flourish under Burebistas, but it is difficult to say whether it was due to a direct decision of the King or to the political conjecture that encouraged the emergence of a strong nobility class around the Mureş Valley. Why would such a large settlement develop in such an inaccessible and unfriendly location? Maybe because it already was a sacred place of utmost importance for the Dacians.

In Burebistas' time or shortly afterwards, Dacians started to build stone citadels in Hellenistic style.

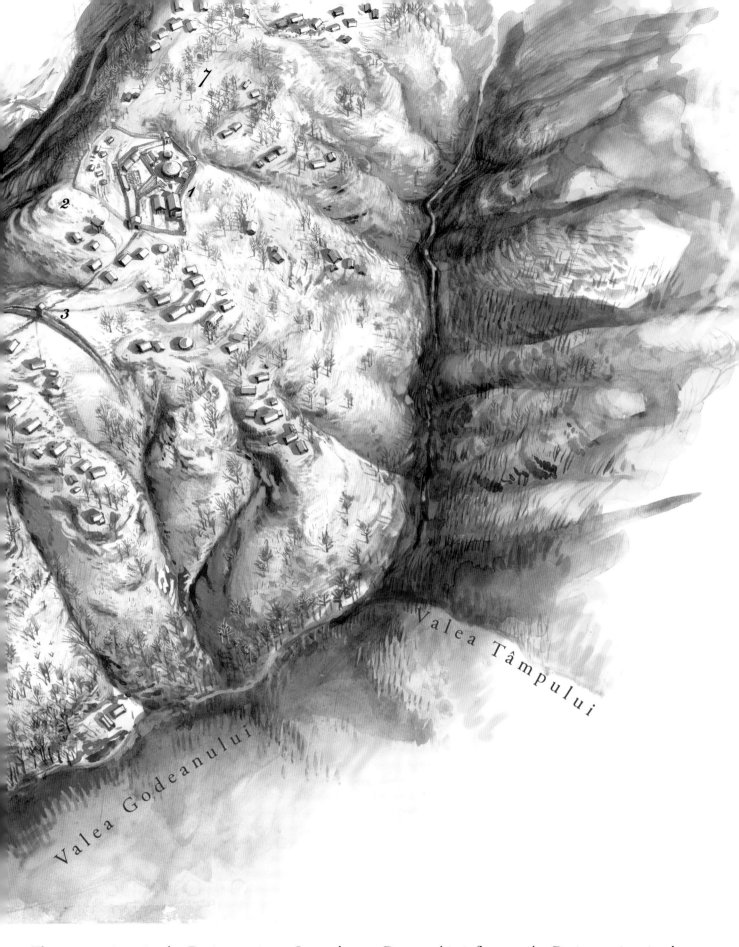

These are unique in the Dacian territory. It can be easily speculated that a Dacian elite came into direct and long term contact with the Hellenistic world – most probably the Greek cities on the Black Sea shore, and then tried to copy the same type of civilization in the Dacian mountains.

Due to this influence, the Dacian society in the Orăștiei Mountains was the most advanced in all Dacia and Sarmizegetusa Regia was the largest and most developed Dacian settlement known to this day. Its similarities to Greek communities do not stop at the carved stone walls. Sarmizegetusa Regia had a water

distribution system of burnt clay tubes identical with those in the Greek and Roman world. The few water sources available were collected into the buried tubes and transported to great distance. The pipes were provided with air holes and protected by wooden troughs carved from tree-trunks – half below, half on top of the tube. A collection and decantation barrel was found near the water source know as *La Tău* (At the Pond).

Archaeologists who worked on these terraces found traces of wooden houses on stone foundations and a rich inventory, indicating a high living standard. Among the finds, a huge ceramic vessel stamped in four places with the words "*Decebalus*" and "*per Scorillo*" – translated as either *Decebalus, son of Scorillo*, or "*Deceballus, donated this vessel through (craftsman) Scorillo*". In another nearby house, a set of medical tools was found. They were identical with the Greek or Roman ones, showing that people who lived here had the skills to use them.

The houses had large storage rooms for cereals (wheat, lentil, horse beans, millet). As elsewhere in Europe, grains were kept in special vessels buried in the ground. The settlement may have counted 4,000-5,000 inhabitants. Unfortunately, the traces of these houses are invisible to the public because, after being studied and recorded, the fragile remains (charcoal, foundation stones, nails, staves, pottery shards, etc) were covered with earth. The only visible indication that the houses existed are the horizontal terraces carved into the hill.

Like everywhere in the Orăştiei Mountains, a mature iron-industry flourished. At the Sarmizegetusa Regia settlement archaeologists found metal workshops, many ironsmith tools similar to those used to this day, traces of ore reduction ovens where Dacians created iron in the shape of cakes (blooms) prior to further processing into practical objects. Painted ceramic workshops producing luxury items were unique in the Dacian world.

Collecting archaeological data from Grădiştea Muncelului Hill was and still is a difficult job. The place was systematically destroyed by the Romans. Houses and barracks of the Roman legionaries were erected on top of the Dacian temples, which were torn down. Starting in the 16th century, records indicate that treasure hunters, drawn by rumors about the gold and silver found in the area, rummaged through the ancient ruins. In 1803-1804 a large group of miners and an infantry battalion were brought in by special request from Vienna to look for treasures and the hunt has continued to this very day. The destruction, the complexity of the settlement, the incomplete

Fragment of ceramic pipe with air hole.
It was used to carry drinking water in the Grădiştea Muncelului Hill settlement.
© The Orăştie Ethnographic and History Museum.

Reconstruction of the interior of a Dacian house from the Grădiștea Muncelului Hill.
The household was investigated in 1955 on the western quarter of Sarmizegetusa.

digs, the absence of records and published information extracted by modern time research, especially over the last 30 years, make the archaeological site of Sarmizegetusa Regia one of the most important but least understood sites in Romania.

Without science literature and correct popularization materials, history dilettantes were left to generate endless speculations, some erroneous and some verging on the fantastic. This has provided ample opportunity for mythologizing Dacian culture, rituals and history.

THE SACRED AREA

The terraces in the Sacred Area conceal many secrets. The area still awaits extended digging, for a better understanding of the ground plan. It is yet unclear whether it was an open space or it was surrounded by walls. Visible ruins of five temple structures suggest that Dacians were polytheists although a monotheistic culture is also taken into account.

The presence of a strong wall on the south-facing side, reinforced with three clearly identified towers, strongly suggests that a fortified enclosure existed around the sacred area. Otherwise, what would have been the point in building military towers to reinforce

a wall that did not enclose anything?[2]

Two of the few water sources on these hills sprang on the sacred terraces, where they were collected and used for worship; then they were directed to the houses below, through buried ceramic tubes.

Four-sided temples had roofs, possibly steeply-pitched to allow snow to slide down, but no walls. They were open wooden structures, with the roofs held by columns that we may imagine sculpted, maybe even painted. The columns lay on massive circular stone foundations, some weighing several tons, that prevented the heavy frame from sinking unevenly into the ground, tilting and finally falling over. These stone foundations are the only ones visible now, although originally they were partially buried. Older temples were made of limestone blocks and more recent ones of andesite, a volcanic granite quarried 70 kilometers away (40 miles). The sacred space around each temple was defined by a low fence of vertical stone slabs.

---

2   This theory is not embraced by many archaeologists, although the proven existence of a massive wall reinforced with towers suggests an enclosure. It is true, the enclosure has not been discovered, but neither has anyone looked for it.

Reconstruction of the Sacred Area monuments.

The archaeological site has been researched since prior to WW-II. However, it still remains largely unknown, due among other things to the difficult environmental conditions (isolation, climate); the huge amount of earth to be removed; the digging methods used at the dawn of Romanian archaeology; and, last but not least, the incomplete or superficial recording and publishing of the results of the research. Expert consultant for the reconstruction: arch. Anişoara Sion.

This hypothetical, incomplete reconstruction, with numerous blank areas, is based on information published so far.

1. Traces of metal shops and ore reducing ovens; large amounts of iron tools in store. **2.** Dacian terrace wall of unknown length. In front of it, on the 10th terrace, two older phases of the construction, also Dacian. After the conquest, Romans made serious interventions by leveling and consolidating the 9th terrace. Complex traces of an important Roman residence. **3.** The Great Andesite Temple, whose disk-shaped bases measured over 2 meters (6 feet) across. The bases were aligned on four rows of 10 discs each. It is believed that the monument was never completed. The war stopped the construction short. **4.** On the corner of the 10th terrace, three adjacent buildings of different periods, unclearly and incompletely documented. One of them is built in the murus dacicus technique. Roman intervention is visible. **5.** Supporting wall between the 10th and the 11th terrace. It was doubled in order to sustain the colossal weight created by the Great Andesite Temple (3). **6.** The sacred road, paved with limestone slabs, was partially unearthed and restored on a 50 m (150 feet) portion. It is not known exactly where it started or whether it split towards the 10th terrace as well. **7.** Paved square at the end of the sacred road. **8.** The square andesite temple I. A limestone podium led to the entrance. The small pillars lining the sacred space and the bases of the columns (most of them gone) are made of andesite. **9.** The square andesite temple II, similar to the former. The bases are tall andesite cylinders, most of them preserved (6 x 3 rows). A water collection channel comes from under this temple after/before passing under the "Andesite Sun". **10.** The Small Round Temple, over which Romans erected another building. **11.** The Great Round Temple. **12.** The Small Limestone Temple. Probably dismantled before Decebalus' time. It had 3x6 column foundations. No small pillar enclosure was found. **13.** The Great Limestone Temple, the last Dacian phase. **14.** Access stairway from the valley. Assuming this was an enclosure wall, such a gate would require a watch tower to protect it. **15.** Strong wall on which three towers were identified, one of them pentagonal. The presence of defensive towers suggests that an enclosure did exist, but its outline is completely unknown.

Terasa a VIII-a

1

Terasa a IX-a, amenajată de romani

2

Terasa a X-a

6

Izvor existent şi în antichitate

Construcţie insuficient s...

12

13

14

Sca...

4

3

8

9

10

Terasa a XI

5

11

7

?

*...elar
...publicată*

*Canal de drenaj din
blocuri de calcar*

15

Turnul pentagonal

*Turn dispărut în epoca lui Duebal.
Desființat cu ocazia construirii
templului cu 60 coloane   (vezi esplicațiile)*

...ces

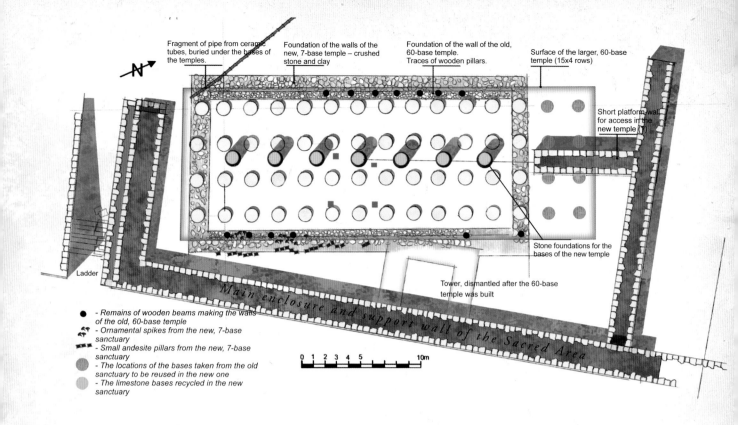

Fragment of pipe from ceramic tubes, buried under the bases of the temples.

Foundation of the walls of the new, 7-base temple – crushed stone and clay

Foundation of the wall of the old, 60-base temple. Traces of wooden pillars.

Surface of the larger, 60-base temple (15x4 rows)

Short platform wall for access in the new temple (?)

Stone foundations for the bases of the new temple

Tower, dismantled after the 60-base temple was built

Ladder

Main enclosure and support wall of the Sacred Area

● - Remains of wooden beams making the walls of the old, 60-base temple
- Ornamental spikes from the new, 7-base sanctuary
- Small andesite pillars from the new, 7-base sanctuary
- The locations of the bases taken from the old sanctuary to be reused in the new one
- The limestone bases recycled in the new sanctuary

0 1 2 3 4 5   10m

THE GREAT OLD LIMESTONE TEMPLE

A circular temple exuding mythical rituals intrigues tourists who come to see the Sacred Area of Sarmizegetusa. It is the Great Limestone Sanctuary (Temple), also known as the "Old" one, or "Burebistas". Archaeological research identified three separate building phases of this edifice.

The columns of the initial temple rested each on four stone blocks, not on a round stone foundation. In a second phase, the temple had four rows of 15 round stones supporting as many wooden columns. A long time after it was built, the temple was dismembered and seven of the limestone bases were used for a new building, erected one meter above the old one. Unlike temples, it had wooden walls and a single central row of columns running under the ridge of the roof. After the Roman conquest, Roman buildings were erected on the ruins of this edifice.

The old temple with 60 limestone bases

The new temple, with 7 limestone bases

Wood Pillars in the wall of the large 60-base temple was built

Enclosure andesite pillars

Stepping level of the 7-base temple

Carbonized traces of wooden columns

Foundation of the walls and andesite columns of the new temple

Tower, dismantled after the large 60-base temple was built

Bases of the first temple

Stepping level of the first temple, with no round bases

Base foundations Layers of stone and clay

0 1 2 3 4 5m

A reconstructed section of the Great Limestone Temple in two separate phases (see the plan above). On the left, the phase of the building with 60 stone bases, on the right the more recent phase, with 7 re-used bases and small andesite pillars about 1 meter (3 feet) higher. The bases themselves stood on stone and clay foundations.

Colum bases of the Old Great Limestone Temple in the 1981 arrangement (restoration). The middle row, with stone foundations, belongs to the 3rd phase of construction, the most recent one.

Andesite bases (over 2 m/6 feet diameter) of the Great Andesite Temple on the 10th terrace. They were very well preserved because, unlike limestone bases which are sensitive to water and to soil acids, andesite is practically everlasting.

THE GREAT CIRCULAR TEMPLE

This temple included a sacred space enclosed by two circles of andesite pillars. In the middle, at 3.5 meters (11 feet) from the inner circle, was the wooden temple, plastered with clay. Archaeologists found the circular print of 84 wooden pillars buried up to 1.5 meter (5 feet) deep into the ground. They rested on stone bases that prevented them from sinking. Above the ground, the pillars were probably 2.5- 3.5 meters high. The circular wooden wall was plastered with a thick layer of fine clay.

The clay must have burned during the wars with the Romans, making archeologists believe at first that walls were covered in some sort of tiles. There were four entrances with stone thresholds and hinged doors decorated with large ornate metal spikes (treated with a sort of transparent enamel as a protection against rust). The roof could only be conical, a feature common to the wider Thracian and Germanic cultures.

Another construction lay inside the circular temple was - an apsidal space with two entrances. The general resemblance of this temple with the houses of metal workers living on mountain tops (at Rudele or Meleia) could suggest that a crafts-god was worshipped here.

An unfortunate "reconstruction" by a Communist-era film crew of the Great Circular Temple in the 80's, implanted vertical wooden beams of various sizes meant to indicate the highest and lowest possible height of the original wooden pillars. It failed to offer any explanation to what was being represented. As a result, subsequent generations of visitors are confused by what they see and discussions are fueled regarding Dacian "mysteries."

The same thing happened with the number of short stones surrounding the Temple. After digs in the 50's and 60's, all this became the object of complex mathematical calculations and speculations about a calendar temple which were then challenged when a new count was determined in 1980-1981.

THE "ANDESITE SUN" ALTAR

The sacred monument, apparently having multiple functions, consisted of a central disc and 10 rays, like cake slices, all carved in andesite. The "Sun" was seven meter across and it was continued by a "ray" of limestone blocks, protruding out of the circle for 9.5 meters (31 feet). It was probably used for astronomical measurements (the shadow the wooden indicator, the *gnomon*, was measured on it). The visible andesite structure rested on a double foundation: two layers of limestone blocks. Inside the foundation, a limestone vessel carved in the shape of a basin with a spout collected liquids from sacrifices, libations and other rituals, as well as the water used to clean the altar. Once the basin filled, it overflowed through the spout into a collecting channel hidden under the rim of the Andesite Sun. The channel itself was an exceptional piece of work, being carved in limestone. It also collected the water of the 11th terrace, the one with the temples, and exited the Sacred Area across the defensive wall, through a huge andesite trough, today lost.

THE GREAT ANDESITE TEMPLE

Researchers agree this was the most recent Dacian temple in the Sacred Area and that it was destroyed before completion. Situated on a higher terrace than

Structure of the andesite altar known as the Andesite Sun. 1. *Central disc, 1.46 m/4.79 feet, on a square foundation of recycled limestone blocks;* **2.** *Andesite segments with rectangular orifices disposed in a circle. White marble and limestone mushroom-shaped pieces of about 12 cm/5 inches (**2'**) fit into the orifices. It is unclear what they were used for;* **3.** *Rammed yellow clay and crushed stone;* **4.** *Foundation of recycled limestone blocks;* **5.** *Orifice in the andesite segment directing liquids into the limestone basin (on the left, the original piece, extracted from its location and thrown near the altar);* **6.** *Channel from U-shape carved limestone blocks;* **7.** *The "Limestone Ray".*

the circular temple, it was the endpoint of the first part of the sacred path, suggesting that Dacian priests and master architects wanted it to impress the viewers.

Earlier, the site was occupied by a smaller temple surrounded by small limestone pillars. But recent evidence shows that, for the first time in the Orăştiei Mountains, a monument with stone columns, instead of wooden ones, was planned here. Enormous andesite foundation stones over 2 meters (6 feet) wide supported smaller column bases on top of which stood andesite

columns made of 2 to 4 smooth cylindrical blocks of stone. Had the temple been completed, scores of andesite foundations would have been found (assuming that even if they destroyed the temples, the Romans could hardly have taken away such stonework). Only eight or nine have been found so far, not all of them of the same size. It is hard to imagine the considerable efforts Dacians had to put into transporting these huge massive andesite stones from quarries 70 kilometers away (42 miles) close to today's city of Deva.

Reconstructed section of the 10th and 11th terrace. *The height of temples and walls is hypothetical.*

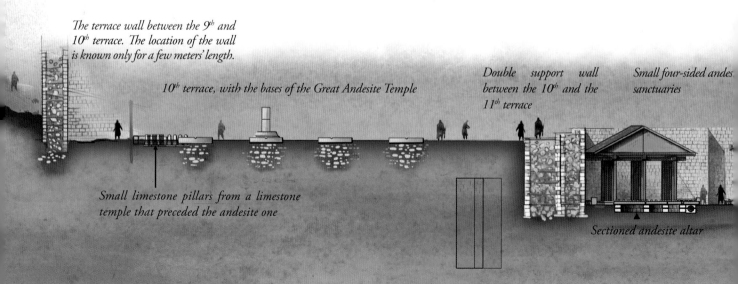

The terrace wall between the 9th and 10th terrace. The location of the wall is known only for a few meters' length.

10th terrace, with the bases of the Great Andesite Temple

Double support wall between the 10th and the 11th terrace

Small four-sided andes sanctuaries

Small limestone pillars from a limestone temple that preceded the andesite one

Sectioned andesite altar

Pentagonal tower.

THE CITADEL

Fortifications in the central part of the Grădiştea Muncelului Hill remain a complicated puzzle, very difficult to research. The stone citadel on the hill is in fact a Roman construction[3] built after military units (*vexillarii*) belonging to several legions were based here. Most probably, the unusually shaped camp was erected only after the second Dacian war, in 106. Which one, then, was the citadel of Sarmizegetusa, meant to protect the Dacian capital and to give a hard time to besiegers? Could Sarmizegetusa have been an open, unprotected settlement? I for one do not think so. Though archeologists disagree on this point, most probable is that the Sarmizegetusa citadel protected the Sacred Area. The idea is backed up by the observation that the massive walls supporting the ninth terrace, the one withholding most of the Dacian temples, have towers on the inner side. Three have been clearly identified: two rectangular and one pentagon-shaped. No one would build towers on a wall unless it enclosed an area that required protection.[4]

Unfortunately, archaeological digging stopped at the end of the wall. In the early 1990's, Professor Ioan Glodariu suggested, based on the traces of a former wall, that the Dacians had a citadel on top of the "nipple" (the phrase belongs to C. Daicoviciu) on the upper side of the Roman fortification. He also maintained that the royal fortification of Sarmizegetusa Regia (*Basileion*) was a

small and modest fort, with no towers, no strategic value and no notable finds inside except a watch tower of stone and wood. Others strongly disagree with this hypothesis even if a small fort did exist on top of the hill.

For more validation that a strong Dacian citadel enclosed and protected the Sacred Area, digging needs to resume in several locations and the results of the research to be made public.

FEŢELE ALBE

A steep valley separated the civilian settlement on the sunny terraces of the Feţele Albe (White Faces) Hill from the Grădiştea Hill. In the place known as the Şesul cu Brânză (Cheese Plain), archeologists

---

3   This fact known to archaeologists for a long time was not made known to the general public, rather, it was restricted to scientific papers, due to ideological pressures. It was not acceptable that the fortification from the Dacian capital should not be Dacian (see page 136)

4   At Costeşti, the stone walls do not enclose the whole top of the hill, but are completed by earth and wooden walls.

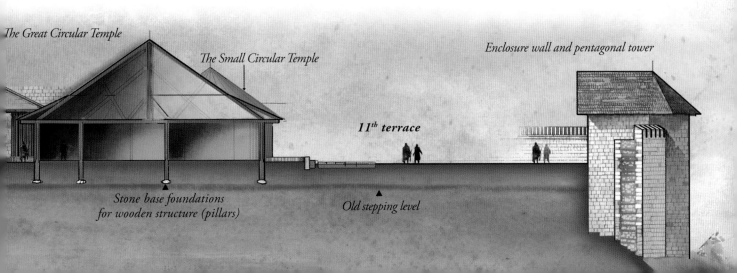

The Great Circular Temple

The Small Circular Temple

Enclosure wall and pentagonal tower

11ᵗʰ terrace

Stone base foundations for wooden structure (pillars)

Old stepping level

unearthed a group of terraces supported by stone walls, water drains and ceramic tubes, a round sanctuary and houses built with great care for quality. It seemed to be a religious or housing complex for the elites, or maybe even the royal family. There appear to be no protection elements, at least from what is known at the current stage of the research.

THE IRON CIVILISATION

Archeological teams who started working at the Dacian citadels in the Orăştiei Mountains before and especially after WW-II were surprised to learn that a genuine iron industry flourished in the area. At the Sarmizegetusa Regia settlement, on Grădiştea Hill, substantial evidence of metal workshops was found, as well as thousands of very diverse iron objects in various stages of completion. Nowhere else in the Geto-Dacian lands had such large deposits of raw iron, iron bars and iron objects been found. The more research advanced, the clearer it appeared that the whole of south-western Transylvania (including Poiana Ruscăi Mountains and the Hunedoara area), but particularly Sarmizegeusa Regia and the surrounding fortifications, operated the largest iron-making center and biggest ironsmith workshops not only in Dacia, but in the entire "barbarian" Europe (north of the Roman Empire's Danubian boundary) from the 1st century BC until Trajan's conquest.

It is hard to say what exactly led to such a boom in this area, but it is quite sure that iron-making was the base for an explosive economic and military development of the Transylvanian kingdom. It is very possible that the evolution of metallurgy also

Hypothetical reconstruction of a blacksmith's workshop at Sarmizegetusa Regia.
*The rammed clay hearths were raised from the ground. Archaeologists found that the earth
underneath was burned red deep down; proof that they were used for a long time.*

Iron tools storage, discovered in 1952 on the 8th terrace, also named the Workshops Terrace. Eight separate groups of iron blooms and tools were found in this area. The largest amount was found in and around a cauldron made of iron sheet (left) and included: blacksmith tools (tongs, hammers, mallets, anvils, rasps, etc), carpentry tools (axes, saws, chisels), agriculture tools and a few weapons (a total of over 180 objects, right). Photos reproduced from the 1953 report "The Grădiştea Muncelului Archeological Digs" - Constantin Daicoviciu and his collaborators in Studii şi Cercetări de Istorie Veche (Ancient History Studies and Research).

had a very strong religious component, such as a central cult for some god similar to the Greek Hephaestos. It is clear that ironsmith workshops were a monopoly of the king and military elites and an important source of revenue.

Some Dacian kings were wise enough to invite foreign craftsmen mastering the advanced technologies of the Greek and Roman world, offering them generous payment and other advantages. Ironsmiths must have been invited alongside Greek architects, stone workers and masons to help build such impressively-sited citadels around the capital. We have reasons to believe that many foreign craftsmen worked in the Sarmizegetusa region during and after Burebistas' reign. They could have been Romans allured by good gains or craftsmen sent by Domitian after the peace treaty with Decebalus. In their workshops, many locals must have learned the trade. The proof of their connection with

Greco-Roman ironworkers (who could be of any ethnic background, for that matter) is the similarity between the numerous tools found with the Dacians and the Greco-Roman ones. They are often identical and marked with Greek letters. Many other items - like compasses, found solely in Sarmizegetusa and nearby - are specific for the Roman world or imported from there.

"The iron ore could be found in great quantities in this area. It was extracted at the surface and processed in the vicinity of quarry. Traces of iron smelting furnaces were found everywhere in Dacian settlements. In these furnaces, the ore mixed with wood charcoal was fried at high temperatures (obtained by using bellows to inject air). As a result of this process, an iron cake was formed at the bottom of the furnace". [5]

5   Borangic Cătălin – "Făuritori de arme. Metalurgia nord-dunăreană între specializare şi necesitate" in *virtusantiqua.ro*

Dacian iron tools discovered at Grădiştea Muncelului.

Right: *blacksmith tongs found at Grădiştea Muncelului / Sarmizegetusa Regia.*

Both photos: George Nica © - MNIR, Bucureşti.

These iron cakes named blooms, similar in shape and size to round loaves of bread, were 99% pure iron. The material could not be used as such for weapons and tools because it had no resistance and rusted immediately. The smiths needed to put it through a heat treatment process called carburization, followed by quenching.

Traces of slag from ore reduction were found in many locations, including in the round dwellings on high mountain tops like Meleia, Rudele and Pustâiosu, where seasonal communities of blacksmiths worked. On the terraces on and around the Grădiştea Hill, scores of iron blooms were found in underground holes; they weighed an average of 10 kilos (22 pounds) each, but the largest of them came close to 40 kilos. In total, several tons of smelted iron were found in this area.

An amazing amount of iron objects was also found in the Orăştiei Mountains. It is clear that the industry was providing finished goods of excellent quality for a whole region. Just before and during the Roman wars, a huge quantity of weapons must have been produced here. But weapons were immediately delivered to conflict zones explaining why not so many of them were among the finds.

Blacksmiths must have worked around the clock during the wars against the Romans. Their tools and iron appeared to have been hid in haste before they hurriedly left the besieged forts carrying only the basic tools in their arms or on horseback.

Apparently, the blacksmiths did not come back for their tools and iron. They were found by archaeologists (or, sometimes, by archeological poachers) 1,900 years later. The deposits included over 27 anvils, sledge hammers, hammers of various shapes, bellows lids, chisels, rasps, wedges, iron rakes, etc. Traces of the forging furnaces such as slag or metal drops were found around the workshops. Sets of tools for woodworkers (carpenters, wheelwrights, barrelmakers who were probably the most common craft in the area) were found by the scores: adzes, hatchets, saws, axes, drawing knives, drills, chisels; agriculture tools: scythes, sickles, coulters, pruning knives, hoes; hammers and other tools for stone cutters; various household objects: knives, barbecue spikes, tripods, hoops for barrels, scissors, crampons for footwear (only in

even the famous *falces*, the scythe-like Dacian swords, could be found, except for two at Sarmizegetusa.

The making of helmets required exceptional skill and expertise, but there is little doubt that Dacian craftsmen were able to craft such elaborate products. The best proof are the well known discs ("shields") found at Piatra Roşie, where the most valuable find was not gold, but an iron treasure.

In 1948, archeologists dug up remains of a richly decorated wrought iron disc, with a wild boar in the center. The disc was restored, inexactly, as it turned out, and exhibited for 50 years as a Dacian parade shield. In the first years after 2000, one of the archeological looter groups left to roam freely across the Orăştiei Mountains citadels with metal detectors found another set of iron discs. They were stacked in a hole made by the Dacians next to the apsidal building. The rust had welded the discs together and the poachers broke some in their attempt to separate them. It is not clear how many discs there were exactly, but somewhere between seven and ten. These items entered the international antique market and until 2013 only three of them have been recovered by the Romanian authorities. Two are at the

the mountain area); metallic parts for constructions and furniture and ornaments and so on. Iron elements of harnesses and spurs were also found, as well as weapons: spears, arrow heads, long Celtic swords, short pointed swords similar to Roman ones (*gladius*), curved blades for breaking Roman shields (*falces*), sickles to fix on the wheels of war chariots, short daggers (*sicae*) displayed by nobility, and iron disks placed in the center of the shields to protect the warrior's hand (*umbones*), also used to hit the enemy. Although it is almost certain that armor was also produced here – mail shirts and helmets worn by military elites – such items are impossible to trace today because they were the most prized trophies. It's no wonder, since not

Dacian iron sickle found during illegal digs in the Orăştiei Mountains.

Previous page, bottom: Dacian iron rake found in the tool deposits of the Orăştiei Mountains. These rakes were used mainly in agriculture, but they might have been used for pushing coal, in metal works.
©- The Orăştie Ethnographic and History Museum.

National History Museum in Bucureşti and another, broken in two, at the Transylvanian History Museum in Cluj alongside other fragments discovered in 1948. More are expected to be brought back to Romania.

Different in details, these discs are part of a unitary series. Each one bears the very realistic representation of an animal in the middle: wild boar depicted in different ways, as well as lion, griffon, and a sort of long-necked goat with a short nuzzle. The general style of the representation is tributary to Greco-Roman classical art. The technique of shaping red-hot iron by hammering required tremendous dexterity for such a complex relief. It indicates exquisite craftsmanship, even at the level of the iron industry in the Orăştiei Mountains.

Iron disk found at Piatra Roşie. Detail of a European bison.
Photo: Marius Amarie. ©-MNIR Bucureşti.

TRAJAN'S WARS AGAINST DECEBALUS

It is well known that most contemporary writings on the Dacian Wars were completely or partially lost over time. Centuries of fires and destruction in Europe - especially in important cities, where libraries were located - and the scarcity of copies or late transcripts resulted in very few and fragmented testimonies.

This absence of written sources is compensated by numerous Roman monuments dedicated to these wars: Trajan's Column, *Tropaeum Traiani*, sculptures of Dacians, the Great Trajanic Frieze as well as archaeological sites uncovered in countries where the conflicts took place (Romania, Bulgaria, Serbia).

Emperor Trajan inherited the Dacian crisis from his predecessors. He understood that the source of conflict emanating from that territory had to be put to rest once and for all. It was evident to him that neither Dacia's status as a client state nor King Decebalus' personal status as a friend and ally of Rome, both obtained as part of the treaty negotiated with Domitian, were guarantees of a lasting peace. Those conditions had favored the Dacian King. This was especially true since the military power and economic prosperity of his land, the largest and strongest kingdom north of the Lower Danube, was partly due to the Roman monetary *stipendium* paid every year to Sarmizegetusa. Rome's long-standing trading relationship with Dacia also fueled the Kingdom's development.

What worried the Romans, and particularly Trajan, was that Decebalus' army, trained by Roman officers and technicians who came to Dacia after Domitian's peace treaty, and additional large number of deserting legionaries turned mercenaries, would sooner or later

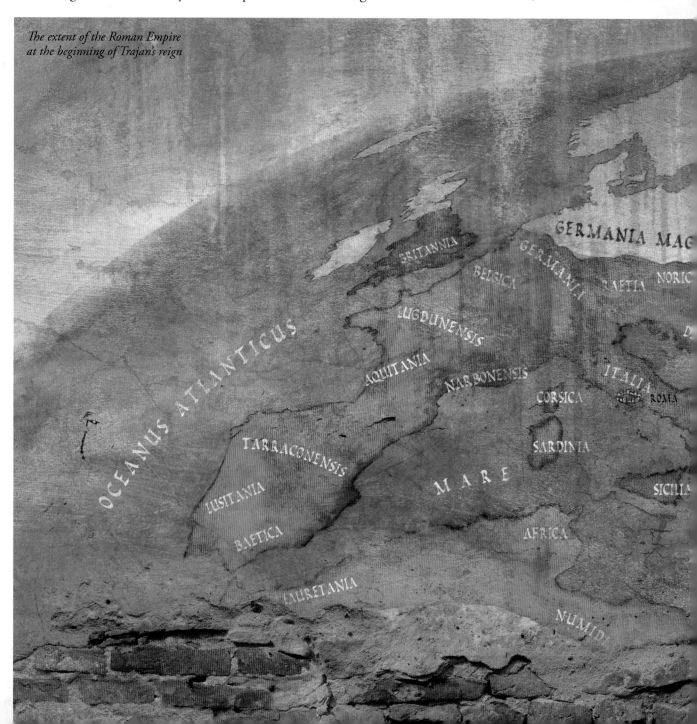

The extent of the Roman Empire at the beginning of Trajan's reign

become an increasingly dangerous enemy, rather than a trusted ally.

In short, Decebalus' Kingdom was a threat. It had become a political, economic and military power that could no longer be tolerated on the borders of the Empire. It was clear that a traditional enemy could not be allowed to gain force, day by day, not to speak with the help of Rome.

Cassius Dio observed the constantly growing power and arrogance of the Dacians. Other ancient authors spoke of the "Dacian threat" and "Decebalus - the foe", though probably under the influence of imperial propaganda. But no particular or immediate incident is known that could have served as a pretext for starting the war. For Decebalus the situation was changing. He happened to need peace and failed to react aggressively even when the regular annual client-state payments stopped coming from Rome.

Settling the score with the Dacians for the never avenged defeats suffered during Domitian's reign may have prevailed in Trajan's mind. The memory of humiliating defeats and of fake triumphal parades had to be erased along with Domitian's name. Alluding to these parades, Pliny the Younger wrote about "*imitations of triumphs*" for "*victories that had been faked*" as well as about huge sums paid by Domitian to the Dacians only to be allowed to appear as victor[1].

We don't know for sure, but it's very possible that Decebalus, who was a wily diplomat and strategist, was forging a huge barbarian coalition against Rome thus triggering Trajan's reaction. An anti-Roman alliance must have already been in place, because there is no other way to explain how large armies of

---

1 Pliny the Younger in Trajan's Panegiric.

Dacians, Sarmatians, and other warriors living outside Decebalus' kingdom could be mobilized so swiftly and efficiently to attack Moesia Inferior months after Trajan launched his offensive in Dacia. This would also be the only available explanation for Decebalus' relation with the king of Parthia[2], Rome's archenemy in the Middle East. Moreover, Trajan's plan to conquer the Parthian kingdom and possibly the East could not exclude Dacia, and thus allow it to become a potential "stab in the back".

Therefore, as soon as he became Emperor, Trajan forsook Augustus' geopolitical thinking that held Roman expansion to the lengthy borders of the Danube River. He launched an attack against Dacia with a goal of annexing and annihilating the King's center of power in Sarmizegetusa. It was the first time in its history that Rome sought to annex territories north of the River. It is probable, too, that Dacian controlled natural resources, including abundant gold, silver and salt, found almost exclusively north of the Carpathian Mountains, played a significant part in influencing his decision to turn Dacia into a province[3].

How large was Decebalus' kingdom? Until recently, it was believed that it roughly matched today's Romania in size, perhaps even larger. But now it is known that Romania's territory was inhabited not only by Dacians and Getae but also tribes of Sarmatians and Bastarnae in what is present-day Moldova, not to mention in Dobrogea. The region was divided between several Dacian or Getic kingdoms, not always at peace with one another. At the time of the Roman wars, the strongest Dacian Kingdom was the one in Transylvania, ruled by the King from Sarmizegetusa. It's hard to say which of the Dacian rulers mentioned by ancient documents were seated in Sarmizegetusa. But to come back to our initial question, we definitely know that Decebalus controlled the land inside the Carpathian arch, encompassing Transylvania and the Apuseni Mountains, plus the Maramureş and Banat regions, spreading south of the Southern Carpathians, into Mehedinţi, Gorj, Vâlcea, Argeş, Prahova, Buzău

and the northwest. The Dacian tribal fiefdoms in Moldova were probably not under his direct authority. But Decebalus, who maintained relations with the king of Parthia, must have mastered a system of alliances that brought all neighboring barbarian kingdoms, be they Dacian, Getic, Sarmatian or Germanic, under his indirect control.

The news of Emperor Nerva's death in 98 AD reached Trajan at *Colonia Claudia Ara Agrippinensis* (today's Köln), in *Germania Inferior*, brought by *Publius Aelius Hadrianus* (who would later become Emperor Hadrian). Nerva had good reasons to choose Trajan for his successor. His fame as an army commander and the respect of his soldiers weighed a lot in his decision. By that time, Trajan already had in mind an attack against Dacia and was determined to continue the anti-Dacian policy initiated – but never accomplished – by Domitian.

Domitian was the one who had brought four legions to Dacia's frontiers fifteen-years before. He had also increased payments for Roman legionaries. In many ways, he had set the stage for Trajan's campaigns. In 99, Trajan inspected the frontier (*limes*) of the Lower Danube provinces and started maintenance works at the Danube fortifications and access roads. He also decided to reduce the *stipendia* to Dacia or even cut them altogether.

Between 98 and 100 AD, a rock-hewn road along the Danube River Gorges was completed and re-paired. The works had begun in Tiberius' time and were continued by Vespasian and Domitian. At the same time, a channel was dug alongside Danube, at Šip (Serbia), to allow Roman vessels to avoid the dangerous whitewaters in the gorges (later known as the Iron Gates). The Danube fleet, until then split in two – upstream and downstream of the Gorges - was expanded and reorganized.

According to the rules of the war, the invading army needed to be twice as large as that of the invaded enemy. Historians concur that the Roman army was huge for that time; the numbers ranged

---

2 Parthia, a powerful Middle East kingdom neighboring Persia.

3 Looting Transylvania's natural resources and the famed treasures of the Dacian kings in order to solve a so-called economic crisis in the Roman Empire is very unlikely to have been the main reason for invading and annexing Dacia. This old theory, now completely abandoned by researchers, was a cliché promoted in the 1950s and a modern myth typical for the anti-imperialist historiography of that time. It went along well with Ceauşescu's national communist views, proving how greedy Roman invaders were. Trajan's time, however, was the most prosperous period of the Empire, who did not necessarily need the Dacian gold. Any speculation in that respect is an ideologically motivated historical fake.

between 60,000 at the beginning of the wars and 140,000 at their peak. There must have been fewer troops in the first campaign against the Dacians (101-102) than in the second (105-106). To face these armies, Decebalus had about 35-40,000 fighters, not counting external allies – Dacians, Sarmatians or Roxolani and other Germanic tribes.

EXPEDITIO DACICA PRIMA

Troops were mobilized from all parts of the Empire to be garrisoned on the southern right-bank of the Danube. Legions III Flavia Felix, based in Singidunum (Belgrade), and VII Claudia had been deployed in Moesia Superior (northern Serbia) since Domitian's time; in Moesia Inferior (north-western Bulgaria and Dobrogea), Vespasian had deployed Legions I Italica (at Novae, today Svištov, Bulgaria) and V Macedonica (based in Oescus, today Ghighen, Bulgaria).

Legions I and II Adiutrix[4] and XIII Gemina were summoned from Pannonia province, along with many other *vexilarii* from Germany and from across the whole Empire. A total of 13 or 14 legions – in their entirety or just parts of them, are estimated to have taken part in the Dacian Wars. Numerous other units supported them: *alae* (cavalry units), regular auxiliary cohorts and irregular ethnic troops from client states, including Syrians, Moors, Berbers, Suebi, Iberians, with their own weapons and equipment.

---

4   Adiutrix legio (pl. adiutrices legiones). Both Legions I and II were adiutrix, "auxiliary"; after the Dacian war, Legion I Adiutrix also received the name Pia Fidelis - "devout [and] faithful".

In 101 AD, Trajan left Rome on the 25th of March, heading for Moesia Superior. Relief carvings on Trajan's Column in Rome show the Danube shores and guard towers exchanging signals with fiery torches. Traces of such towers have been found on the Serbian side, around Clisura Dunării, as well as in Dobrogea. Forts were stocked with provisions and gathered troops awaited for the signal to cross over.

Dacian topography was no secret for Roman generals. They surely had a good sense of the rugged and mountainous topography gathered during Domitian's campaigns. The Roman army also included mercenary Dacian soldiers as well as connections with traders who knew the land and language well. Combatant forces were accompanied by their own support army of engineers, architects and military technicians coordinated by Apollodorus of Damascus himself. A book entitled *Polyorketica* (*Treatise of war machines*) was authored by him on the art of siege aided by technology and war machines.

Balbus, one of Trajan's chief *gromatici* (surveyors, named after the surveying instrument, the *groma*), wrote:

"But after we set foot on enemy land [...] our Caesar's military operations soon required the science of measurements [...] As for the plans of the bridges, even if the enemy had wanted to harass us, we were able to indicate the width of rivers from our side. The divine science of numbers showed us how to measure the height of mountains that needed to be conquered".

The Roman army was way too large to invade from one direction. It was split into three, following three different routes that eventually converged on Decebalus' capital, Sarmizegetusa.

The first scenes on Trajan's Column. *Small towers protected by palisades, haystacks and signal towers (with torches on top) are visible along the Danube River, the Empire's northern frontier. Towers were used as guard posts, as fire signal posts and as lighthouses for river navigation. Auxiliary soldiers scan the opposite (Dacian) shore, suggesting that tension was high before the imminent invasion. Etching from Pietro Santi Bartoldi's album, Colonna Traiana, late 17th century. BAR.*

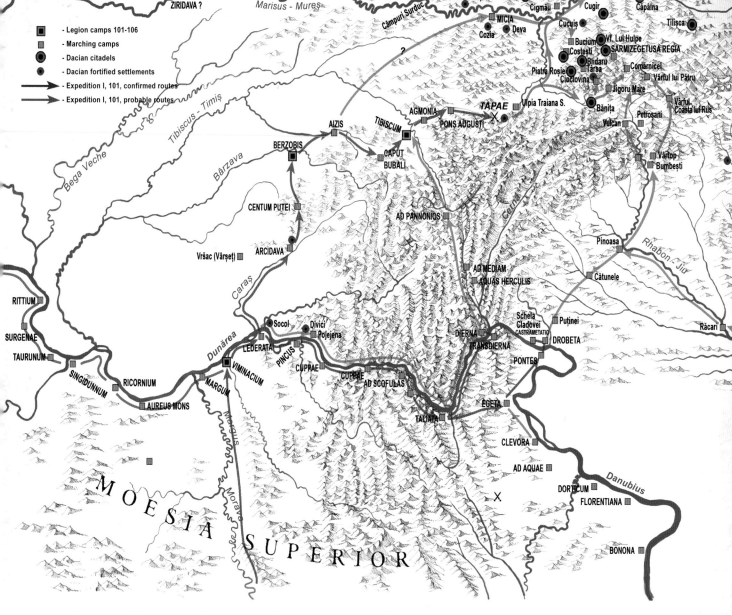

First stages of Trajan's expedition in 101. *The southern routes along the Jiu, Drobeta-Bumbeşti and Oescus-Răcari-Bumbeşti-Sarmizegetusa, were probably used later in the 102 campaign. Perspective view from the south-west.*

The column led by Trajan himself, accompanied by Praetorian prefect Claudius Livianus and other generals such as Licinius Sura or Glitius Agricola, started from Viminacium (today Kostolac, Serbia), a Danube River port in Moesia Superior where Legion VII Claudia was based. A first pontoon bridge of interconnected vessels was put up downstream from Viminacium, next to the Lederata camp (Rama, Serbia), allowing troops to cross the river. The route followed by the Emperor is known due to the only remaining fragment from Trajan's *Commentaries ("… from there, we advanced to Berzobis and then to Aizis")*. The Romans marched through Flumen, Arcidava, Centum Putei, Berzobis, Aizis, Caput Bubali, Tibiscum (Jupa/Caransebeş, Caraş-Severin county). We know these ancient place names thanks to an old map entitled the *Tabula Peutingeriana*. It is also probably the itinerary illustrated on Trajan's Column. At Berzobis, in the Banat plains, a huge camp was built for Legion III

Flavia Felix led by General Pompeius Longinus, the unit that would later occupy the Banat and Haţeg Country.

With the stone-carved cliffside river roadway and the canal built to avoid the waterfalls in the Danube Gorges, army purveying became highly efficient. The Danube fleet was now able to navigate without encumbrance up and down the river, bringing in supplies and soldiers.

We can only guess the invasion routes of the additional armies as no actual proof exists. A possible direction, accepted by most historians today, was across the river at Dierna (Orşova), where the Danube receives the waters of the Cerna, and then up this tributary or up the Timiş River to the Tibiscum camp, where it could join Trajan's column. From there, the two groups could have marched together along the Bistra River to Tapae.

Another possible route could have started in Drobeta, where legions could have crossed on a pontoon bridge, marching to the Jiu Valley, across the Vulcan Mountains on old mountain plateau trails cutting through the village of Jieț and to the Streiului Valley.

Traces of a huge marching camp were found in Schela Cladovei, a suburb of Drobeta. The earth camp could have been built for this occasion or, more probably, kept as a bridgehead on enemy land ever since Domitian's time. It was represented in 17th century etchings by Marsigli under the name of Castrametation and was probably used as a resting place for legions coming across the river.

A third possible invasion direction in 101 could have been the one taken by Legion V Macedonica and other units camped in the Danube port of Oescus. Under the command of Manius Laberius Maximus, Governor of Moesia Inferior, they possibly crossed the river at Sucidava (today in the town of Corabia), where the Romans had established a bridgehead, and marched along the Olt River upstream in an attempt to confront a potential threat at Buridava (now Ocnița, in Vâlcea county). The city was the center of the strongest political entity south of the Carpathians and a traditional client of Rome.

There seems to have been limited resistance, if any, while Roman legions crossed the Danube and then northward into the Carpathian Mountains. The only incident is mentioned in one sentence in Criton's *Getica* and since it was written by Trajan's doctor we may assume it happened when the Emperor crossed into Banat: "*Even as they were crossing, and while they set foot ashore, they were attacked (by the Dacians)*". The lands between the Danube and the Carpathians, outside the authority of Dacian kings in Transylvania, had long ceased to be a danger to the Romans. Most former *davae* in the plains had been deserted or destroyed decades before (or as late as Domitian's wars) and the rest had been reduced to mere commercial towns with no military function. Following Domitian's wars, the Dacian side of the Danube River was completely demilitarized and controlled by the Romans as a result of the peace terms. In the Carpathian foothills a few Dacian fortress sites survived (Polovragi, Buridava, Cetățeni, Pietroasele), probably under Sarmizegetusa's control, but without strong fortifications.

Thus started the greatest and costliest war Romans ever fought, the war involving the highest number of troops and covering the largest area. Superlatives could go on, since the conflict led to the building

Part of the Danube Gorges called "the Large Cauldrons". In ancient times, the level of the water was about 30 m lower. View from the Serbian (right) shore, upstream. Photo: Andrei Posmoșanu..

of the largest bridge in Europe to that date, the largest triumphal monument (*Tropaeum Traiani*), the greatest plunder of precious metals, the greatest monument built in Rome, with the highest number of statues ever sculpted to depict the vanquished. And probably the highest number of victims on both sides.

The military goal was to annihilate the power of the Dacian Kingdom, concentrated in its sophisticated network of mountain fortifications, genuine eagle nests. The larger goal was destroy the political and religious center in Sarmizegetusa Regia.

The swift progress of Trajan's armies through Dacian territory did not cause their generals to let down their guard. They all had in mind the mistakes made by their predecessors during Domitian's campaigns. So troops only marched on relatively short distances of 30 km (18 miles) per day and constantly reinforced their rear, considered conquered territory.

We gain a picture of how Roman army advanced by reading the description made by Flavius Josephus in *The War of the Jews*, a campaign some thirty years earlier in 66–74 AD.

"(Emperor Vespasian) ordered those auxiliaries which were lightly armed, and the archers, to march first, that they might prevent any sudden insults from the enemy, and might search out the woods that looked suspiciously, and were capable of ambuscades. Next to these followed that part of the Romans which was completely armed, both footmen and horsemen. Next to these followed ten out of every hundred, carrying along with them their arms, and what was necessary to measure out a camp withal; and

after them, such as were to make the road even and straight, and if it were any where rough and hard to be passed over, to plane it, and to cut down the woods that hindered their march, that the army might not be in distress, or tired with their march. Behind these he set such carriages of the army as belonged both to himself and to the other commanders, with a considerable number of their horsemen for their security. After these he

Crossing the Danube on a pontoon bridge.
During the 101-102 war, Romans must have
built at least three such pontoon bridges, one
in the plains of Banat, at Lederata, one at
Drobeta and another at Oescus-Sucidava.
The boats used for the bridge are reconstructed
after examples on the Column.

marched himself, having with him a select body of footmen, and horsemen, and pikemen. After these came the peculiar cavalry of his own legion, for there were a hundred and twenty horsemen that peculiarly belonged to every legion. Next to these came the mules that carried the engines for sieges, and the other warlike machines of that nature. After these came the commanders of the cohorts and tribunes, having about them soldiers chosen out of the rest. Then came the ensigns encompassing the eagle, which is at the head of every Roman legion, the king, and the strongest of all birds, which seems to them a signal of dominion, and an omen that they shall conquer all against whom they march; these sacred ensigns are followed by the trumpeters. Then came the main army in their squadrons and battalions, with six men in depth, which were followed at last by a centurion, who, according to custom, observed the rest. As for the servants of every legion, they all followed the footmen, and led the baggage of the soldiers, which was borne by the mules and other beasts of burden. But behind all the legions carne the whole multitude of the mercenaries; and those that brought up the rear came last of all for the security of the whole army, being both footmen, and those in their armor also, with a great number of horsemen". (Book 3, chapter 6, 2)[5]

The huge army could be constantly furnished without any risk of having its supply lines cut. The unusually high number of soldiers made the columns extremely long. Advance guards were sent out during the night to find suitable locations for the next marching camp. By the time the last troops left a camp, the new one was already in place, one day's walk ahead. Historian Titus Livius, known as Livy, wrote:

"Your fathers considered a fortified camp as a harbour of safety in all the emergencies of an army; out of which they were to march to battle, and in which, after being tossed in the storm of the fight, they had a safe retreat. For that reason, besides enclosing it with works, they strengthened it further with a numerous guard; for any general who lost his camp, though he should have been victorious in the field, yet was deemed vanquished. A camp is a residence for the victorious, a refuge for the conquered. [...] This military settlement is another native country to every soldier: the rampart is as the wall of his city, and his own tent his habitation and his home." (Livy, Ab urbe condita, Book 44, chapter 39)[6]

Another interesting excerpt from Flavius Josephus

describes the way Romans organized their camps:

"They divide the camp within into streets, very conveniently, and place the tents of the commanders in the middle; but in the very midst of all is the general's own tent, in the nature of a temple, insomuch, that it appears to be a city built on the sudden, with its market-place, and place for handicraft trades, and with seats for the officers superior and inferior, where, if any differences arise, their

5 All quotes from Flavius Josephus are from "The War of the Jews" translated by William Whiston (1667-1752), the Internet Archive.

6 Titus Livy - "Ab urbe condita", English translation by William A. McDevitte, 1850, the Perseus Digital Library.

causes are heard and determined (…)".

"When they have thus secured themselves, they live together by companies, with quietness and decency, as are all their other affairs managed with good order and security. Each company hath also their wood, and their corn, and their water brought them, when they stand in need of them; for they neither sup nor dine as they please

(Continued on page 84)

The road through the Danube Gorges.
Reconstruction of the cliff carved segment of road built with tremendous effort during the reign of the four emperors. Trajan is the one who completed the road, which went from Singidunum (Belgrade, Serbia) to Bononia (Vidin, Bulgaria).

S I S.

BEN
t. Rom.

MAREKOBILA
Antiq. Rom.

PESCABARA
Antiq. Rom.

Trikule

Via incila rupe lecta

LUKADNITZA
Antiq. Roman.

Poretz

STAREVARE
Antiq. Rom.

GRADANITZA
Antiq. Rom.

GRADISCA
Antiq. Rom.

Poretza

ANTIQU. ROM
Vallum

MIROVA
Vallum Ant. Rom.

PALANKUTZA
Antig. Rom.

Via lapidibus strata. A

ORSO
Antiq. Rom.

ROMAN WORKS IN THE DANUBE GORGES

Meeting the Carpathians, the Danube cuts a long, impressive passage through the mountains. For sailors, it was the most difficult place on the whole course of the river. From ancient times to the modern age, navigating the gorges from one end to another in a larger boat remained an impossible challenge. This was because rocks protruding close to the surface obstructed navigation like reefs. The strong currents churned water and made it look as if it was boiling, hence the name "Cauldrons". These were Danube's

famous cataracts or Iron Gates. The most dangerous place was between Drobeta and Dierna (Orşova), downstream from an island that the Ottomans would centuries later call Ada-Kaleh (Citadel Island) near the former Serbian town of Šip. An insurmountable obstacle, even when waters were high, it forced Romans to keep two fleets on the Danube: one upstream, the Pannonian fleet (Classis Flavica Pannonica), and one downstream, the Moesian fleet (Classis Flavica Moesica). However, just before the Dacian wars

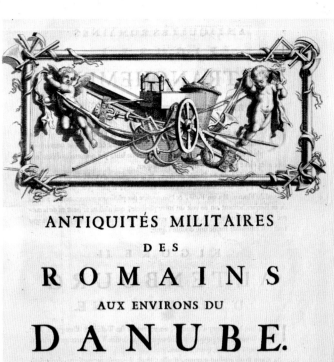

ANTIQUITÉS MILITAIRES

DES

ROMAINS

AUX ENVIRONS DU

DANUBE.

Yant à faire la Description des Antiquités Militaires des
Romains en guise d'Itineraire, ou à mesure qu'elles se pré-
sentent dans l'ordre que je me suis préscrit, je commence par la
Tome II.   A   FI-

Luigi Ferdinando Marsigli (1658–1730), *an Italian aristocrat who served as an officer and engineer in the Habsburg army during Leopold I. An enlightened spirit, eager to learn and interested in natural sciences, geography and archaeology, he recorded his observations during his expeditions along the Danube and published them in his Danubius Pannonicus-Mysicus - a six-volume book lavishly illustrated with over 300 engravings. He left valuable data on the known topography of Roman antiquities in the Danube River basin at the crossroads of the 17th and 18th centuries and is considered to be one of the forefathers of modern archaeology. Above, the title page of the volume on Roman antiquities decorated with a Roman ballista, anchors and construction tools. On the left, detail of the Danube Iron Gates illustration, the first detailed map of ancient (and medieval) fortifications in this area.*

the Romans found a way to navigate the Iron Gate cataracts. A 57 meter wide channel was dug through the wetlands on the right bank. It was protected by 14 meter high walls and its 3,200 meters (9,600 feet)-long course made it possible to avoid the river's churning white waters. The work was mentioned in a 101 inscription found near the village of Carataş (Serbia), stating that Trajan "...ob periculum cataractarum derivato flumine tutam Danuvi navigationem fecit" ("...with the river diverted because of the danger

of the cataracts, managed to ensure navigation all along the Danube").
Traces of dykes protecting the Roman channel were still visible in the 19th century, when Austro-Hungarian authorities built another huge canal in the same place – the Šip Channel, inaugurated in 1896. All those traces are now submerged under the waters of the Iron Gates hydro-dam.

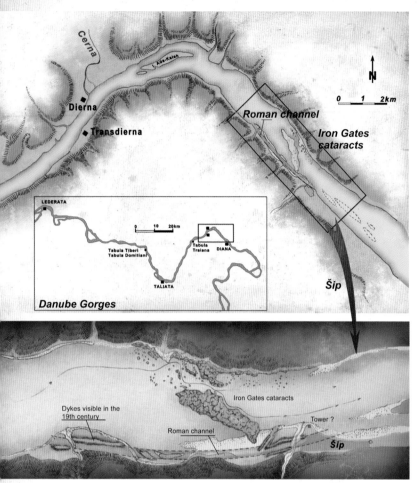

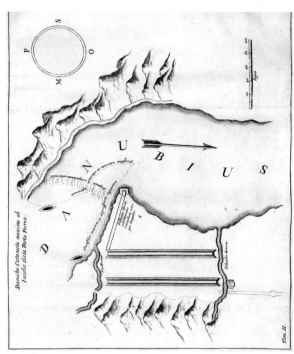

Above: Plan of the dykes for the Roman channel, as still visible in the 17th century. Detail from an etching by L.F. Marsigli.

Left: Localization of cliffs at the Iron Gates cataracts and the 3,200 long detour of the alternative Roman channel.

Downstream from Ada Kaleh Island – whose ancient name is not known – located midway between the Roman camps Dierna (today's Orşova) and Transdierna, one soon reached the Iron Gates cataracts. This was not the only natural obstacle; other cataracts, though less dangerous, waited a few miles upstream. The first Roman emperor to understand the importance of a good road on the right bank of the Danube, linking Singidunum (today's Belgrade, in Serbia) and Bononia camp (today's Vidin, in Bulgaria), was Tiberius, successor to Augustus. Inscriptions from his time prove that Roman engineers – most certainly skilled legionaries – had to overcome extremely difficult conditions to carve a road through the impracticable terrain. The road was further improved during Vespasian's and particularly Domitian's reigns. Austro-Hungarians teams sent in late 19th century to assess the regularization of the river and the new Šip Channel found inscriptions (tabulae) memorializing the works completed under their reign on limestone cliffs bordering the river. One of the inscriptions,

*Iron Gates cataracts. Etching from the volume "**Hungary and Transylvania**" by John Paget, 1855-London. Dan Dimăncescu Collection.*

Cliffs from the Iron Gates cataracts during low waters. 19th century postcard..

The Danube at the "Cauldrons." Romantic etching from "The Danube" by W.Beattie, illustrated by W.H.Bartlett, 1844-London.
On the left side, the Wallachian shore, on the right, the Roman road beneath the limestone walls.
Dan Dimăncescu Collection.

now lost, mentioned works undergone by Legion VII Claudia in Domitian's time to extend and improve a portion of cliff-carved road. Even in his first year as Emperor, Trajan ordered that fortification works on the Danube, initiated by to Domitian, be continued. Roads carved along almost vertical walls of the gorges were widened by a system of wooden-beam supports that practically doubled their width. These were fitted into rock-carved orifices. At the same time, new forts were built and connected to the network of roads, signal towers and lighthouses (round or square), fluvial ports and the Šip Channel.

Two lithographys from "The Danube" illustrated by Adolph Kuniker, 1826 -Vienna.
Left : *Towers on the Roman road.*
Right : *Tabula Traiana, incorrectly represented, or some other inscription. BAR Collection.*

themselves singly, but all together. Their times also for sleeping, and watching, and rising are notified beforehand by the sound of trumpets, nor is any thing done without such a signal; and in the morning the soldiery go every one to their centurions, and these centurions to their tribunes, to salute them; with whom all the superior officers go to the general of the whole army, who then gives them of course the watchword and other orders, to be by them cared to all that are under their command; which is also observed when they go to fight, and thereby they turn themselves about on the sudden, when there is occasion for making sallies, as they come back when they are recalled in crowds also". (Flavius Josephus, Book 3, chapter 5, 2–3)

Details of Dacian battles are available only in the scenes sculpted on Trajan's Column, in scarce surviving fragments from Cassius Dio's historical writings probably inspired by Criton's *Getica*, and a few other disparate sources. Well represented on the Column are actions where the Emperor participated in person. Other events of the invasion were probably less documented, if at all.

What the Column shows us is that the first weeks passed without major events. Legionaries are shown cutting down trees and building roads, bridges and fortifications.

Legionaries, as elite soldiers, were not only involved in sieges but in other large military operations requiring complex engineering works. These disciplined and efficient fighters also intervened when necessary in the battles led by auxiliary forces. The Column highlights their efficient organization, while also sending a message: Rome's armies advancing into the dark, forest-covered barbarian territory bring along civilization. Legionaries are shown laboring in their armor coats (*lorica segmentata*)

Tabula Traiana and part of the Roman road *(photograph from the 1930s).*
Trajan's road works in the Danube Gorges were glorified in a new tabula, the largest, most decorated and best preserved of all the Danube inscriptions. The lower part was destroyed over time by fires lit by Serbian fishermen who used to take shelter under it. Historians managed to reconstruct the text: it tells of Trajan who excavated the rock from the mountain and built the road/bridge with wooden beams. In the 19ᵗʰ century, the title "Tabula Traiana" was added at the top. Yugoslavian authorities saved it from destruction in the 1960s, when they removed it from the limestone wall and raised it 30 meters above the Iron Gate reservoir lake.
Photo: Stelian Petrescu, BAR Collection.

Trajan's road and tabula. Etching by Ludwig Mohn, an Austrian artist from early 19th century. BAR Collection

which seemed unnatural but made them easy to identify as well as glorified them.

The auxiliary soldiers, many of them of barbarian origin themselves, waiting yet to acquire Roman citizenship, were almost never shown as part of the organization and building effort. Doubtlessly, they did take part in the works but showing only Roman citizens was much more compelling and had a far stronger propagandistic function. In order to make Dacians easily distinguishable, they were stereotypically depicted with no protection equipment such as helmets or armors.

The atmosphere of a Dacian war camp is revived in a few lines written by Dion Chrysostom, who traveled to Dacia in 98 AD:

"I (…) came among men who were not dullards, and yet had no leisure to listen to speeches, but were high-strung and tense like race-horses at the starting barriers, fretting at the delay and in their excitement and eagerness pawing the ground with their hoofs. There one could see everywhere

Reconstruction of the Tabula Traiani *with the entire inscription and ornaments. Sculpted in 100 AD, the tabula was decorated with figurative motifs in a naïve, provincial style. The authors were probably legionaries with some artistic talent. The frame was supported by two winged goddesses of victory and dolphins decorated the corners. The tabula was sunk from the vertical plane of the rock and protected by a cornice decorated with rosettes and a spread eagle.*

Trajan's Column. *After the crossing of the Danube, most scenes preceding the Battle of Tapae show Roman armies, particularly legionaries, cutting through forests, building roads, bridges, camps and other fortifications. The message needs to be read in terms of propaganda. The onlooker had to understand that legionaries did not just complete military tasks. They brought Roman technology and civilization into the Dacian mountains, albeit by force.*

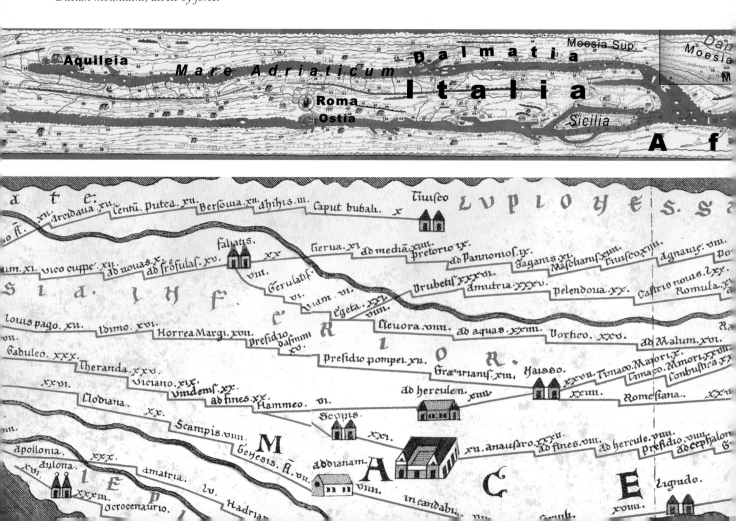

swords, everywhere corselets, everywhere spears, and the whole place was crowded with horses, with arms, and with armed men. Quite alone I appeared in the midst of this mighty host, perfectly undisturbed and a most peaceful observer of war, weak in body and advanced in years, not bearing 'a golden scepter' or the sacred fillets of any god and arriving at the camp on an enforced journey to gain a daughter's release, but desiring to see strong men contending for empire and power, and their opponents for freedom and native land." (Dion Chrysostom, Discourses, XII, 19, 20, the Loeb Classical Library)

While the military offensive unfolded, both Trajan and Decebalus were involved in an intense diplomatic war, sending envoys and ambassadors meant to delay the fighting as long as possible. These exchanges increased after the battle of Tapae. In one peculiar episode, a Buri envoy (Buri were a Germanic people, north-western neighbors and probably allies of the Dacians) brought Trajan an unconventional message, described by Cassius Dio:

"When Trajan in his campaign against the Dacians had drawn near Tapae, where the barbarians were encamped, a large mushroom was brought to him on which was written in Latin characters a message to the effect that the Buri and other allies advised Trajan to turn back and keep the peace." (Roman History, Book 68, 8, 1, the Classical Loeb Library, 1925)

Most scholars identified the episode as Scene IX of on the Column, where we can see a barbarian of unusual appearance, poorly dressed, one shoulder bare, falling from his mule at the sight of the Emperor. It is surely not a Dacian[7], but a messenger of the Buri, as mentioned by Cassius Dio, delivering his call for peace on a carving of hoof-fungus.

7   Not to be mistaken for the Buri (buridavensi), Dacian tribe, who lived in what is now Oltenia (western Wallachia) and had their center at Buridava.

Tabula Peutingeriana

This exceptional document is in fact a medieval, 11th-12th century copy of an ancient map, showing the main settlements and the road network during the Roman Empire and beyond, into the 3rd century (or 5th, according to some scholars). Its name comes from the owner of this rare chart, Konrad Peutinger of Augsburg, in whose library it was discovered in the 16th century. The map was made of 12 pieces of parchment (one lost) sewn together to make a 6.80/0.34 m (20/1 feet) strip, kept in a roll. Six of the pieces are reproduced here, covering the area between Italy and the Middle East. The map is an extraordinary source for Dacian history because it mentions most Roman towns (true, sometimes with a changed name), roads and distances (in Roman miles, 1 mile= 1.5 km). The settlements in Dacia, as shown on the map, are those of the 2nd century. It helps us follow the possible routes taken by Trajan's armies, finding which settlements they could have reached and how far apart. For a better understanding of the topography, I have indicated today's names of the main geographical areas, otherwise difficult to identify. Below, a detail of the map, showing Dacia and Moesia. The Eastern Carpathians are named the Bastarnae Alps. Reproduced after Konrad Miller's facsimile, Stuttgart, 1887.

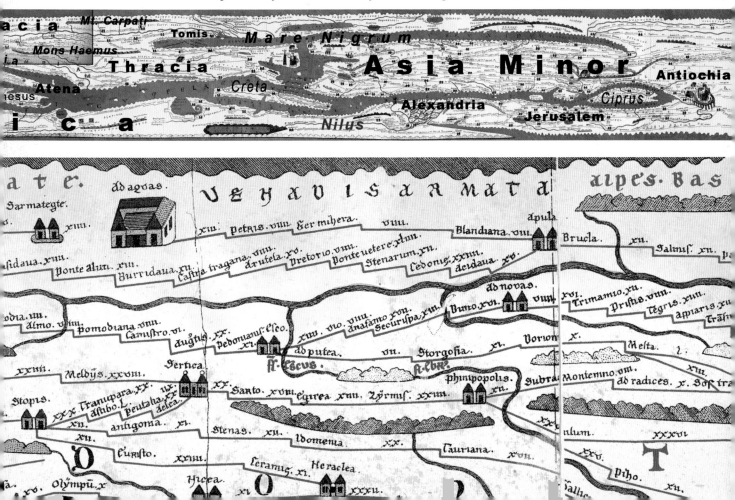

indicators and archaeological traces, the battle could have taken place at the narrow mountain pass known as the Iron Gate of Transylvania, connecting the Banat to present-day Hațeg Country and thence to Transylvania. From Tibiscum, the Roman armies marched up the Bistra River, where they built two camps: a very large one of over 15 hectares (38 acres) in Zăvoi[8] commune and another thought to be somewhere around Băuțari village, according to the *Tabula Peutingeriana*. The former was identified as *Agmonia* (*Agnaviae*, in *Tabula Peutingeriana*); the latter as *Pons Augusti* (Emperor's Bridge), providing evidence that Trajan's itinerary went this way. Traces of ancient, mediaeval and even modern WW-I and WW-II fortifications with earth walls and ditches were found not far from the place where the Bistra River meanders to the right and roads, modern and ancient, start upwards towards the Iron Gate pass. The medieval ones dated from the 16th and the 17th centuries, when the Banat was an Ottoman Pashalik and the region was a constant war zone.

Later fortifications are complex, but they stand

TAPAE

The precise location of the first and most important battle between Trajan and Decebalus is not known. Most authors agreed that according to topographic

8   Not far from the Zăvoi camp, near the village cemetery, Roman thermal baths were unearthed after 2009. The ruins of another small camp, a castellum, were found a few kilometers south of the commune, in the village of Voislova. However, it is highly improbable that this is Pons Augusti.

The Battle of Tapae, *scene XXIV. On the right upper side, Jupiter Tonans controls the battle and supports the Romans by throwing bolts of lightning against an enemy commander. Reproduction from one of the "Die relief der Trajanssäule" albums published by Conrad Cichorius in 1896-1900.*

on top of two ancient earth ramparts. From the left-side hill (to the north, as you look towards Transylvania, suggestively called Culmea Cătanelor (Soldiers' Mount), an earth rampart and ditch go down the slope for 852 meters (2,800 feet), the modern road cutting across them.

The Roman army could have well traveled around the Iron Gate pass, both by the north, on plateau trails, and by the south, where satellite images indicate some fortifications of unclear date. In either of these cases, the fight would have taken place somewhere in the mountains that separate the Banat from the Hațeg.

Not all historians agree that Tapae was on the Bistra Valley; some argue it could have been on the Mureş Valley or in the Hațeg Depression. In Domitian's time, Romans had defeated the Dacians in the same spot, but failed to capitalize on their victory.

On the Column a fierce battle is depicted involving, on the Roman side, only auxiliary troops, including bare-chested barbarians, probably Suebi from the Rhine. As Cassius Dio puts it:

"[Trajan] saw many wounded on his own side and killed many of the enemy. And when the bandages gave out, he is said not to have spared even his own clothing, but to have cut it up into strips. In honour of the soldiers who had died in the battle he ordered an altar to be erected and funeral rites to be performed annually." (Roman History, Book 68/ 8, 2, the Classical Loeb Library, 1925)

Some historians consider this excerpt not to be about Tapae, but about the costly and blood confrontation at Adamclisi, far in eastern Dacia, where, indeed, the Column shows many wounded legionaries. Dio Cassius' original writings have not survived, only excerpts copied by monk Xiphilinus which are believed to have mixed up the chronology of the events, thus supporting the Adamclisi argument. This author believes that while the Column shows no legionaries in metal and leather armors, the fragment does describe the Tapae battle which indeed would have been bitterly fought. The Column scene shows Jupiter *Tonans* ("The Thunderer") supporting the Romans by throwing flashes of lightning (originally painted on the stone) towards the Dacians, who suffer heavy losses. The target of Jupiter's flashes seems to be a young, beardless Dacian nobleman carried by other two soldiers– perhaps one of the notable victims of the battle or even the Dacian commander.

Toward the left, Trajan is offered two decapitated Dacian heads, possibly of high rank. One sees, too, a Roman auxiliary soldier in the heat of battle holding a severed Dacian head in his teeth. It could be the portrait of one particular soldier, legendary for this terrible way of fighting. Auxiliary soldiers were recruited from barbarian lands and it is understandable that some of them kept their habit of cutting their enemy's heads and displaying them as war trophies. On the other side, Dacians seem to have engaged their elite troops, armed with the same weapons as the Romans. Between the trees, their dragon-tailed *draco* flags flutter next to a *vexillum*, a hanging down standard similar to the Roman ones. Here one sees Decebalus watching in his first identifiable representation on the Column. Dacians withdrew before total defeat to organize stronger resistance in the mountains, behind the ring of fortifications surrounding Sarmizegetusa.

This Roman victory was extremely important and Trajan was saluted as imperator by his victorious army. Romans were now free to enter Transylvania across Hațeg Country. To ensure the protection of this strategic point, a marching camp was most probably built on the site of what would become the future capital of Roman Dacia, Ulpia Traiana Sarmizegetusa. From here on, hard work awaited the Roman army. If the south and west of Dacia had not presented them with dangerous situations and stone fortifications to besiege, Transylvania did.

The region was well protected, with many

The Battle of Tapae. *On one side, right under the probable portrait of Decebalus, a young* **tarabostes** *(Dacian nobleman) is carried away from the field after being injured or even killed by Jupiter's lightning.*

hilltop strongholds, some of them reinforced by the very Roman craftsmen sent by Domitian after the peace treaty. Decebalus' soldiers were hardened men, well trained and equipped with both Roman weapons and their own specific Thracian weapons. Mercenaries of various ethnic backgrounds, including Roman and Greek, probably fought alongside Dacians. As Dio Cassius wrote:

"For he had been acquiring the largest and best part of his force by persuading men to come to him from Roman territory." (68, 9, 6)

After the Tapae battle, the Column includes a scene that deserves special attention. Trajan comes to the gates of a major Dacian citadel – as indicated by the *draco* flag fluttering on top of its walls. A bridge crosses a ditch-moat to get to the gate tower. The slope in front of the citadel is protected by pits with wooden spikes and beams. This type of complex fortification, maybe inspired by Domitian's own engineers, was meant to prevent the enemy from bringing siege machines or cavalry too close to the walls. A row of human heads on pikes are displayed on the battlements, next to a *vexillum*. Most historians linked this scene to information provided by Dio Cassius: that Trajan found in a mountain citadel weapons, war machines, prisoners and standards captured from General Fuscus in Domitian's time and never fully returned after the ensuing peace treaty. But the column does not show any Roman victims inside the walls, nor does Dio Cassius

The Battle of Tapae details.
Top: *A Roman auxiliary soldier attacks while holding the severed head of an enemy in his teeth. On the left, a bare-chested Germanic warrior, a Suebae, brandishing a martel.*

Bottom: *Group of Dacian warriors, among whom two stand out - one wears his hair in a band and the other has a protective coat, probably leather-styled armor. Digital coloring is hypothetical.*

Portrait of a tarabostes (Dacian aristocrat) in the Tapae scene. Almost certainly Decebalus' first portrait on the column.

write anything about macabre trophies. The flags could very well be Dacian, not Roman and there is no certainty that the heads belonged to Roman soldiers at all, much less to Fuscus' troops some 20 years earlier.

In the foreground, Roman auxiliary troops are seen setting fire to a Dacian village while a group of inhabitants run away. The fact that villages surrounded the citadels has been confirmed by archaeological research.

If after the Tapae battle, wherever it occurred, the main army led by Trajan came up the Mureş River, the head-topped citadel must have been somewhere on the way to Grădiştea Valley, maybe in Deva. Evidence of an ancient Dacian fortress existed at some point on Deva Hill, but was destroyed when medieval fortifications were built.

With the area that would later become Ulpia Traiana Sarmizegetusa secured by at least one camp, the Roman army started to prepare for winter and to organize the spring sieges. As the story unfolds on the Column, it shows envoys of three different ethnic groups. Judging by the clothes and the Suebian-knot-hairstyle, Trajan receives a representative of the Germans (which included the Buri[9], Decebalus' allies). Behind him, an embassy of

The Battle of Tapae, detail. *Dacian warrior fighting with a Roman* ***gladius***. *Textual and archeological evidence indicate the Dacians used weapons comparable to Roman ones.*

9   The auxiliary troops of German barbarians on the Rhine, who fought bare-chested in Trajan's army, were part of the same large ethnic group – the Suebi. Their name was preserved to this day, under the form *Schwaben* (Romanian: şvabi).

The Iron Gate of Transylvania Pass *(Bucova village) and the remains of barrier fortifications found here. The oldest earth ramparts and ditches (traces of wood and earthen walls) are most probably Dacian. The fortifications were repaired during the fights against Ottomans in the Timişoara Pashalik (17th-18th centuries). After sketches by Hristache Tatu and Dan Oltean.*

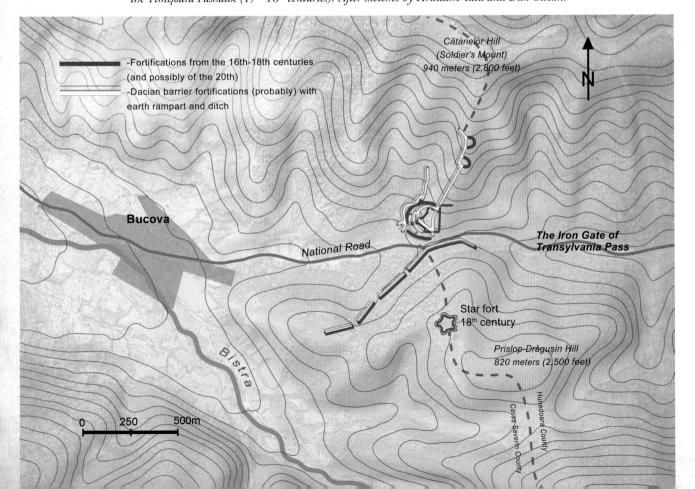

-Fortifications from the 16th-18th centuries (and possibly of the 20th)

-Dacian barrier fortifications (probably) with earth rampart and ditch

Cătanelor Hill
(Soldier's Mount)
940 meters (2,800 feet)

N

Bucova

National Road

The Iron Gate of
Transylvania Pass

Star fort
18th century

Prislop-Drăguşin Hill
820 meters (2,500 feet)

Bistra

Caraş Severin County

Hunedoara County

0   250   500m

Hypothetical reconstruction
of the Battle of Tapae, based
on Trajan's Column

Trajan in front of a Dacian citadel, heavily protected by a trench, by ditches lined with stakes and by tactical passages. Enemy skulls are displayed on top of the walls.
Auxiliary troops set fire to the settlement below the citadel, while Dacians withdraw to the right. The vexillii (vertical flags) were also used by Dacians. Scene XXV.

Bottom: Detail of the citadel, with a draco standard, a vexillum, a guard post tower on high pillars and a round enclosure.

mounted barbarians are gathered, hard to determine if Dacians or Sarmatians. A third group comes before the Emperor in front of a marching camp. This time, it is Dacian *comati*, simple folks, in their typical tasseled cloaks, pleadingly presenting their peace offer. Trajan, in control and seemingly offended by the low rank embassy, ignores their request.

While Trajan marched across Banat towards Tibiscum, the Governor of Moesia Inferior, general Manius Laberius Maximus, left Oescus with a mighty army that included parts of Legions V Macedonica and I Italica plus many auxiliary troops and marched up the Olt River valley, making peace with Dacian leaders in Buridava[10]. Archaeological findings show that the peace may have saved the city from destruction. To keep an eye on the area, the Romans built a camp on the banks of the Olt; it received the same name, Buridava, and in time developed into a thriving city and military base.

After building the camp near Buridava, the Roman army crossed the Carpathian Mountains on plateau trails that followed the Olt River. Later, Romans would carve out a roadway into the narrow, rocky river valley as they had done in the Danube gorges.

After the siege of an unidentified citadel in Transylvania, still far from the Orăştiei Mountains, Maximus captured Decebalus' sister, who was probably married to an important chieftain. There are no details on the capture, but Cassius Dio's testimony could be linked to one scene on the Column, showing Trajan as he leads a woman to an anchored vessel. She carries a child in her arms and is accompanied by a large number of other women who bid her good bye.

---

10 At Ocniţa/Ocnele Mari, county of Vâlcea, a large and prosperous *dava* was dug and researched. It has fortifications, an acropolis and a civilian settlement and was probably the biggest Dacian city in the southern Carpathian foothills, still alive at the time of the Roman wars. The prosperity of the place was surely related to the salt deposits and the trade relations with the Romans on the other side of the Danube. Most researchers identified this city as Buridava.

But why was Trajan on the Danube? We knew him to be in Hațeg, preparing to winter after seizing, as Cassius Dio puts it, *"some fortified mountains"*. (History of Romans, 68, 9, 3). Before the cold season, war came to a standstill[11]. An unwritten rule said that no army ever fought in wintertime.

Apparently, the rule was not always observed. Hundreds of miles away from Sarmizegetusa at the mouths of the Danube on the Black Sea, barbarian kings, Sarmatians, Roxolani, Dacians of Moldova, Suebi, all of them Decebalus' friends, crossed the frozen river in several places. As in the past, when these raids were more regular, endless columns of mounted warriors – some accompanied by their families and convoys of carts – attacked Roman forts on the southern bank and destroyed everything in the way. History left us the names of two Sarmatian commanders who were part of this impressive military diversion: Sardonius and Susagus, old friends of Decebalus', but, apparently, also of the Romans.

Germanic people allied to Decebalus?

Who were the barbarian warriors taking part in the Moesia campaign alongside the Dacian king? It has been established that the coalition included Dacians from

northeastern Dacia (Moldova) and Roxolan Sarmatians. But things are less certain when it comes to Germanic tribes. Did substantial Germanic forces join Dacians and Sarmatians into Moesia? An intense and unresolved debate has long unfolded surrounding the ethnic origin of these Germanic troops. **Bastarnae,** one of the oldest Germanic populations, lived for four centuries (2nd century BC to 3rd century AD) in the north-eastern part of the Dacian territory between the Carpathian Mountains and the Dniestr River. Their existence has been confirmed by both written sources and important archaeological evidence. They probably took part in the Dacian war, although there are no written sources to confirm it. In the 3rd century AD, Bastarnae are often mentioned as permanent fighters against the Romans, alongside the Sarmatians and Carpi. We may therefore admit that the bare-chested warriors represented on Tropaeum Traiani could be Bastarnae.

Another Germanic tribe, the ***Buri***, is mentioned by Cassius Dio in an episode preceding the battle of Tapae, when Trajan received a letter from them and other tribes, advising him to turn back. Scholars place the Buri, who were part of the larger Suebi group, somewhere between the Northern Carpathians, the Middle Danube and the sources of the Tisza River – therefore in today's Slovakia, close to the Polish border. There are no satisfactory explanations for how and why these tribes would have

---

11 Romans ended their war season in October and started it in March (the month of Mars, the war god). Both moments were marked by religious ceremonies (source: virtusantiqua.ro).

Roman iron helmet
(Weisenau type) from
Trajan's time, with two iron
bars crosswise across the skull
to protect it against the downward
strike of the curved Dacian sword, the
falx. This very effective innovation introduced
during Trajan's reign is perfectly illustrated by this helmet, the oldest
known so far. It was found at Berzovia (Caraș Severin county).
Photo: George Nica, © MNIR., București

come as far south as Moesia to fight Romans alongside the Dacians and Sarmatians, but still, it would not have been impossible. The bare-chested warriors (a posture called martial nudity), some wearing the *nodus* hairstyle depicted on the Adamclisi metopes[12], are surely Germanic. Dacians, Getae and Sarmatians did not fight naked, but the Suebi tribes had taken this habit from the Celts. The weapons used by the half-naked warriors on the

Adamclisi monument are an object of debate among specialists. They are shown sporting curved weapons, typical for Thracians and Dacians, and were therefore mistakenly identified as such. At the same time, the Column also shows Germanic warriors with *nodus* hairstyles, loose *bracae* (trousers) and bare chests, but they fight alongside Trajan and are probably Rhineland Suebi. It was possible that Bastarnae endured in Moldova, generating a mixed culture of Dacian, Sarmatian and Germanic influence, impossible to identify solely from archaeological evidence. Perhaps it is they who are the

12   See the opinion according to which these metopes could be attributed to a 4th century reconstruction, in the chapter on the Adamclisi Trophy.

The first attempt at reconstructing the colors of the Column was made by italian historian and archeologist Bianchi Bandinelli Ranuccio (1900–1975). He worked on 1/1 scale casts of scenes XXXI-XXXII for a television documentary film in 1971. The painted casts traveled to Romania in the 80s, to be exhibited at the National History Museum in București (MNIR), where these photos were taken. On the left, we may see part of the scene when the barbarian cavalry drowns in the Danube (scene XXXI), followed by the attack of the heavy cavalry of Roxolan Sarmatians and the siege of a Roman camp in Moesia Inferior by troops of the barbarian coalition. The latter use a battering ram symbolically decorated with a ram's head.

mysterious bare-chested, *nodus*-wearing, curved-weapon-sporting fighters depicted at Adamclisi.

The Column also depicts a dramatic episode of the Dacian raids into Dobrogea, one that was brought to Trajan's knowledge although it was not directly connected to the Romans. An army of Dacian and Roxolan Sarmatian riders are seen drowning in the Danube after the fractured ice gives way under them. Their frightened comrades watch powerlessly from the banks and only two men are seen as saved and dragged to the shore. The calamitous event was important enough to deserve a scene on the Column and its dramatic quality was enhanced at the hand of gifted craftsmen who depicted the suffering and fear of the characters in vivid touches. Such drama

and emotion became a useful propaganda tool serving to influence the opinions of Roman citizens. Subsequent scenes show how Roman fortifications south of the Danube were placed under siege. Poorly defended, since most warriors had been mobilized to advance northward into the Dacian mountains, the Roman camps along the Danube are burned to the ground.

The powerful winter attack in 101–102 AD of the barbarian coalition in Moesia, far away from the main center of operations in the Orăştiei Range of the Carpathian Mountains, took Trajan by surprise. He swiftly organized a counteroffensive, leaving a strong army of legionaries in Transylvania to protect the conquered lands and leading an auxiliary force to Drobeta on the

(Continued on page 103)

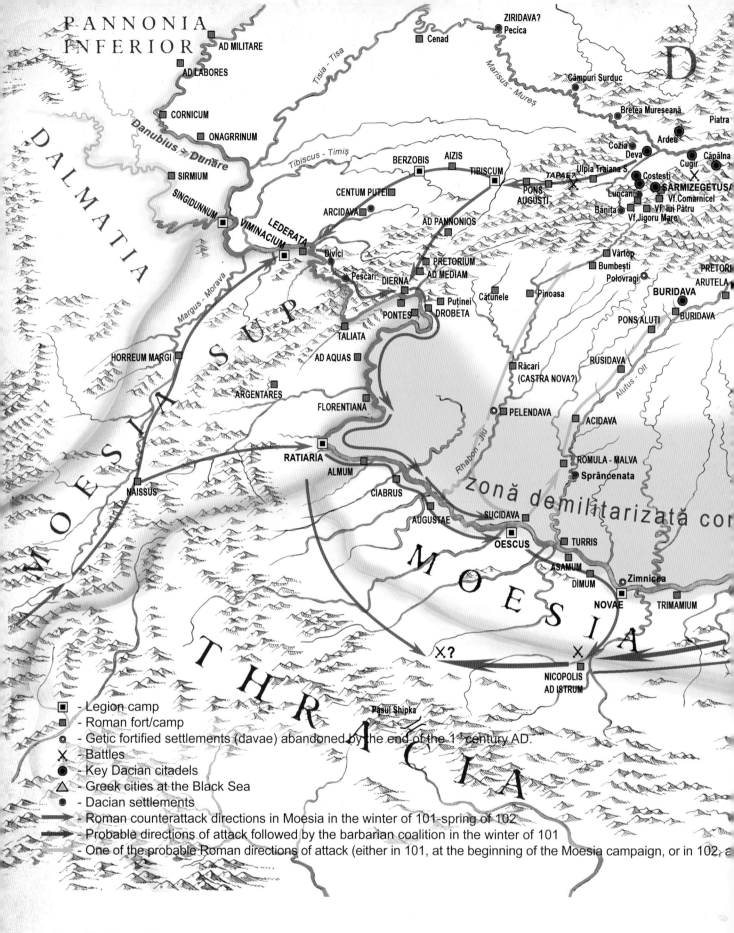

Legend

- ■ - Legion camp
- ▪ - Roman fort/camp
- ⊙ - Getic fortified settlements (davae) abandoned by the end of the 1st century AD.
- X - Battles
- ● - Key Dacian citadels
- △ - Greek cities at the Black Sea
- • - Dacian settlements
- Roman counterattack directions in Moesia in the winter of 101-spring of 102
- Probable directions of attack followed by the barbarian coalition in the winter of 101
- One of the probable Roman directions of attack (either in 101, at the beginning of the Moesia campaign, or in 102, a

The Moesia Inferior campaign. *Winter 101 - Spring 102.*
The possible southern routes used in 102 to cross the mountains are marked in green.

Right: *Hypothetical colors for the episode of drowning troops in the Danube River (scene XXXI).*

CIA

ZARGIDAVA ?
(Brad)

PETRODAVA ?
(Piatra Neamț)

Marisus - Mureș

BASTARNA

Ghindari

Zetea

Racu

Sighişoara   Porumbenii Mari   Odorhei   Miercurea Ciuc

Şeica Mică

Sâncrăieni

Slimnic
terita

Rupea

Alutus - Olt

Hoghiz

Racoşul de Jos

Arpaşul de Sus

Surcea   Moacşa

TAMAŞIDAVA ?
(Răcătău)

Tisești

Covasna

CUMIDAVA

PIROBORIDAVA ?
(Poiana)

ROXOLANI

Cetăteni

Drajna de Sus

Cârlomăneşti

Mălăieşti

Hierasus - Siret

Pyretus - Prut

Pietroasele

Târgşorul Vechi

Barboşi

Tinosul

ARRUBIUM

Piscu Crăsanilor

NOVIODUMUM

TROESMIS

ă de romani de la mijlocul sec I d.Hr.

Bucureşti

Popeşti

BEROE

AEGYSSUS

Naparis - Ialomiţa

ARGAMUM

HALMYRIS

Radovanu

CAPIDAVA

HISTRIA

Căscioarele

Danubius - Istros - Dunăre

TRANSMARISCA

iaria

DUROSTORUM   ALTINUM

TROPAEUM
TRAIANI

TOMIS

PONTUS EUXINUS

FERIOR

CALLATIS

MARCIANOPOLIS

DIONYSOPOLIS

ODESSUS

MESSEMBRIA

The Danube fleet in Moesia Inferior (*Classis Flavica Moesica*) *carrying troops, baggage and horses from the main theater of operations (south-western Transylvania) to the new front opened by the southeastern barbarian invasion. Ice floats on the Danube (it must have been a warm winter). The reconstitution of fluvial war vessels (liburnae) is based on the Column and on the models exhibited at the Museum of Ancient Transport (Museum für Antike Schiffahrt) in Mainz, Germany.*
Right: *Scene XXXIV on the Column. Trajan navigates downstream from Drobeta to a Danube port in Moesia Inferior (Oescus or Novae). Note the various types of fluvial vessels. The Emperor himself steers the admiral-ship.*

Heavy cavalry (cataphract) of the Roxolan Sarmatians, *some of the fiercest allies of the Dacians. They were of Iranian origin and language and led a semi-nomadic life (they lived in tents and left no permanent settlements, only burial sites). Like most steppe warriors, they were great mounted archers. They are mostly famed for their heavy cavalry (cataphract), with both rider and steed draped from head to foot in scaled-armor. The armor sometimes included chain mail and other materials than metal – thick leather, bone or thin slices of horse hoof. They charged with 3 meter long lances. It is believed that some of the equipment sculpted on the base of the Column is Sarmatian (chain mail, helmets). They probably also had draco flags, like Dacians. Sarmatians did not use shields and wore their dagger scabbards tied to their right thigh. On the Column, the Sarmatian cataphract appears in two scenes where horses and riders are excessively covered in scaled-armor (see above, scene XXXI). Trajan's armies must have fought against the Sarmatian cavalry before the Battle of Nicopolis ad Istrum.*

Danube. From there, his naval fleet took his units to Novae, to meet the Dacian and Sarmatian forces. Decebalus' allies had the mission to cut, interrupt or at least destabilize the Roman supply chain to Dacia. In winter time, this would have been a catastrophic blow. Tens of thousands of men were stationed in Dacia and depended upon a constant flow of goods from the Empire.

As Trajan sailed eastward from Drobeta, Moesia Inferior Governor M. Laberius Maximus accompanied by Decebalus' sister was marching down the Olt towards Novae. It was probably there that the young princess was embarked on a ship, in Trajan's presence, and sent to Rome.

The Moesia Inferior Campaign

The violent attacks of the Dacians south of the Danube were the trigger of an apparently minor but illustrative episode mentioned by Pliny the Younger in a letter to Trajan. He tells the story of a Callidromus, slave to Governor M. Laberius Maximus, who was taken prisoner by Sugasus, the Roxolan King, during a raid against a Roman fortress. King Susagus did not keep the valuable prisoner to himself, but sent him, along with other spoils of war, to Decebalus. Callidromus did not stay there long, but was sent all the way to Pacorus II, the Parthian King. Parthians were known as relentless foes of Rome and Decebalus was eager to make new allies for his continued resistance against Trajan. Several years later, the former slave escaped and reached Nicomedia (today Izmir, Turkey), where his story reached the ears of Pliny.

Shortly after Trajan's army reached Moesia Inferior, it engaged in a first confrontation with a body of Roxolan Sarmatian cavalry, possibly an advance guard. The heavy Sarmatian cavalry (*catafracta*) were famous for their long spears and their chain mail armors (of iron, bone and skin and sometimes horse hoof slices) covering both man and horse. Like all steppe warriors, Sarmatians were also excellent horseback archers. It is hard to imagine today how difficult it must have been to fight on horseback without the stirrups (they had not been invented yet, so stability was provided by the saddle only). For the first time, too, the same Column scene shows Roman cavalry.

NICOPOLIS AD ISTRUM

According to the story as told on Trajan's Column, after defeating the Roxolan heavy cavalry, Roman Legions met a massive convoy of raiders at a pass in the Balkan Mountains. A terrible battle ensued, part of it at night time as suggested by the figure of goddess *Nox*, the Night (or *Selene*, the Moon) sculpted at the top of the scene. With the short winter days, her presence is easy to understand. The background shows a row of carts filled with weapons (shields) and other war spoils and two sleeping Dacians by their side.

The Romans won a hard-fought victory. One of the Dacian chiefs of this army took his own life seeing that Trajan's soldiers closed in unavoidably on his troops. This critical success thwarted Decebalus' plan to cut the Roman supplies lines and inspired Trajan to found a new

*Left: **Nomadic barbarians in carts** (most probably Sarmatians, Roxolani) on a metope from Tropaeum Traiani, Adamclisi.*

Bottom: The Battle of Nicopolis ad Istrum. *Upper left, probably to Night Goddess (**Selene** / the Moon), suggesting a night attack against the barbarian camp. A **draco** standard is visible in one of the carts. On the back wheel of the right side cart, one may note a mysterious human bust with broken (or mutilated?) limbs. Scene XXXVIII.*

city. It would be named *Nicopolis ad Istrum*, meaning the City of Victory on the Danube (from the Greek *Nike* – victory). Although the place is miles away from the river, the "ad Istrum" part was added to differentiate it from other settlements of the Empire also named Nicopolis. Trajan remained quartered there for a while, in order to be present at the foundation of the city.

Why a Greek name? Because old Thracia, now divided into Roman provinces, had been for centuries influenced by entrenched Hellenistic culture where Greek was spoken currently alongside local languages. Nicopolis ad Istrum became a thriving city and survived until the devastating 6th century Avar invasions.

Yet, the campaign in Moesia was far from finished. A huge army of Sarmatians, Dacians and Germans crossed the river, probably at Orșova, where Romans had not built any camps yet, and was marching across Dobrogea.

Nicopolis ad Istrum*. The ruins of the city are a few miles north-west from Veliko Tirnovo, Bulgaria.*
Top: *Ruins of the **Odeon**, second half of the 2nd century AD.*
Bottom: *Trajan's name in Greek letters on the pedestal of a statue.*

Tropaeum Traiani*. Two metopes show close combat scenes. The reliefs are rich in details of costume and weaponry and show the fighting techniques of Roman legionaries. However, iconographic information needs to be regarded prudently. Legionaries are shown in heavy armor, scales on the left (**lorica squamata**) and chain mail on the right (**lorica hamata**), with arm protection (**manica**), in striking contrast with barbarians who fight bare-chested and without shields, They must be Bastarnae or Buri, Germanic tribes and neighbors of the Dacians (from whom they could borrow the shape of their weapons). © Adamclisi Archaeological Museum/ MINA, Constanța.*

Night battle at the cart camp. *Both Trajan's Column and Tropaeum Traiani show the carts, indicating that Romans had to confront genuine convoys of barbarians who went to war with their families and all their possessions. The night-time attack below is inspired by scene XXXVIII on the Column; the equipment, weapons and clothing of the Romans and barbarians from the Adamclisi metopes. Barbarians are shown in a didactic selection of tribes. On the right, the Germanic warriors fight bare-chested, wearing their hair in a* nodus, *a knot at the*

temple. However, they use Dacian weapons, as shown on the trophy monument. In the center, one may see a Dacian fighting a legionary, a Sarmatian archer and another Germanic warrior, wounded. The group of heavily armored Romans have their arms protected by metal stripe guards (manicae), as shown on the Tropaeum Traiani.

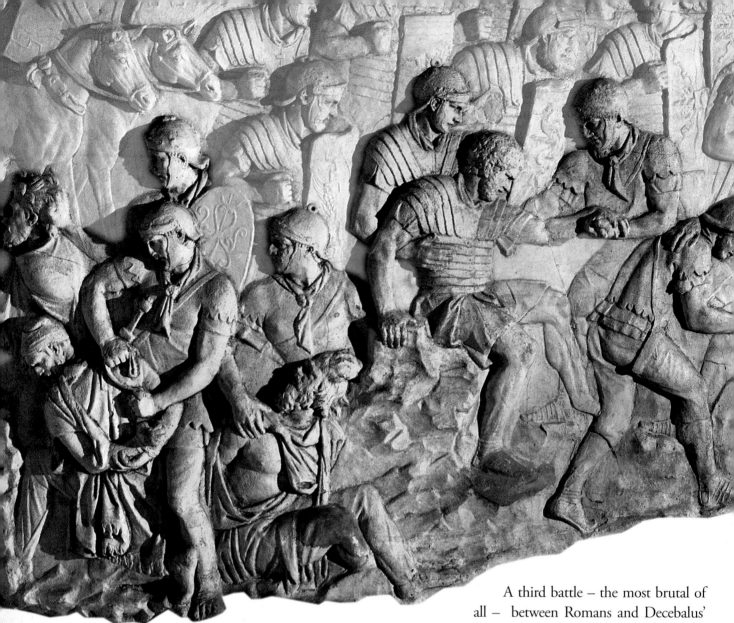

A third battle – the most brutal of all – between Romans and Decebalus' allies was to be fought. Both the Column and *Tropaeum Traiani* amply describe it, but the scenes are very difficult to interpret. We do not know how and where it took place, although we may suppose it was not far from Adamclisi. On the Column, it is the only battle in Moesia where we see both just auxiliary troops and legionaries (Legion XI Claudia?) in their stereotypical armor. The battle was fierce and ended with countless victims on both sides. This can be deduced by the large number of dead Dacians represented on the monument in Rome and by the fact that these are the only scenes depicting wounded Romans. Many barbarian leaders were captured and taken to a Roman fortress. The bravest fighters were honored in a ceremony and Trajan decided to have erected a great triumphal monument memorializing all the battles led in Moesia against the coalition of Dacians, Sarmatians, Buri and Bastarnae. Dedicated

Tropaeum Traiani, Adamclisi. *Battle scene between a Roman soldier in chain mail and three barbarians. They fight bare-chested and with huge curved swords in two hands. Photo: Stelian Petrescu.*

The left side scene is extracted from the marginal space of the third important battle in the Moesia campaign, after the Sarmatian cavalry battle and night battle at Nicopolis ad Istrum. On the left, several barbarian prisoners are brutally bound. They were brought from the heat of battle to which groups of legionaries in the background are headed. Highlighted are two Romans in the foreground, a legionary and an auxiliary soldier who are taken care of after being injured. It's the only scene on the Column where Romans are shown wounded. In the propaganda code of the monument, it indicates that the battle was won with great sacrifice. Detail of scene XL.

Tarabostes wounded to death. *The scene could also show the self-inflicted death of a Dacian commander during the battle of Nicopolis ad Istrum. Detail of scene XXXVIII.*

Most scholars agree that the battle scenes on the Adamclisi trophy describe Trajan's campaign in Moesia Inferior. None of the barbarians in this scene is a Dacian. Although he sports a curved sword and wears a **pileus**(?), this is a Germanic warrior who fights bare-chested, something that Dacians never did. The knotted hair of the dead barbarian in the background confirms the participation of Germanic tribes, although their curved weapons appear to be Thracian. Photo: Stelian Petrescu.

to *Mars Ultor*, "Mars the Avenger," the chosen site was on a hilltop dominating the Dobrogea plateau. It was close to an altar and another mausoleum, probably built in Domitian's time. Again, the Emperor had a city built in the proximity and named it like the monument – *Tropaeum Traiani*.

Trajan was saluted for the third time as *imperator* and minted a gold coin (*aureus*) for the occasion. His victories in Moesia are mentioned by several ancient records, but not in the writings left by Cassius Dio.

It was the time for Trajan to go westward to his main theatre of operations in the Orăştiei Mountain Range. As spring came, the offensive against the fortresses surrounding Decebalus' capital had to go on. At this point, an unusual scene appears on the Column. Three prisoners, stripped, hands tied behind their back,

have their shoulders and chests burned with torches by a few women. Most scholars wrote that the scene showed Roman prisoners tortured by Dacian women somewhere in the mountains. But the scene most likely takes place in Moesia. Since there is no other scene on the Column where Romans are put in inferior or humiliating positions, this is a rare representation. Other historians suggested those were Dacian prisoners, taken as slaves and marked with the branding iron. This fails to explain why the scene is so cruel and violent, which is unnecessary in the case of slaves. The women do seem to be Dacian judging by the dress, which is similar but not identical to the costume of other female characters on the Column known to be Dacian.

Tropaeum Traiani. Metope with two Dacian prisoners, with typical pileus *headwear, probably two commanders, chained together, their hands behind their back. Note their long split shirts. In the background, the Romans soldier wears no armor, only a* paenula, *a woolen cape like a poncho.*

Highly violent and dramatic battle scenes.
Most researchers agree that the last battle of the southern campaign sculpted on the Column was the one in the Dobrogea region, close to the place where the Tropaeum Traiani would later be erected. The battle engaged numerous Roman legions, auxiliary troops, cavalry and Germanic barbarians brought by Trajan from the Rhine area. Dacians and their allies fought bravely, both on foot and on horseback. A group of Dacian riders attacks from the left side, just like the Roman cavalry in the background - indicating that the battle took place on a very wide area. On the right side, nine bodies of barbarians suggest the tragic outcome of the fight. Four survivors flee to the mountains. Scenes XL and XLI.

Dacian women torturing a group of prisoners, burning their naked bodies with torches while their hands are tied behind their back. The troubling and unexplained scene was interpreted by some scholars as representing Roman prisoners tortured by Dacian women. But all scenes on the Column have a propaganda code. Roman soldiers could not have possibly been represented in such humiliating postures. It could be a punishment against traitors or defeated Dacian commanders. Trajan's Column, scene XLV.

The prisoners do not appear to be Roman. Were they Dacian commanders or allies who had betrayed their army and were punished, the humiliation of being tortured by women being so much the greater? Or could they be barbarian chieftains who massacred local populations in Moesia? While there is ample room for speculation, the scene illustrates an actual event whose specifics escape us. Whatever it meant, it reflected an intended propagandistic message. The episode is mentioned because, despite the absence of a full explanation, it provides the image of a brutal war that even involved the female population.

Before the end of the spring in 102 AD, the barbarian coalition troops withdrew back over the Danube. Many of the fighting groups managed to

Reconstruction of the battlefield after the end of the Adamclisi confrontation. The carts shown both on the Column and on the Tropaeum Traiani suggest that some of the invaders were semi-nomadic people. They could only be Roxolan Sarmatians, the most numerous participants in the Moesia campaign after the Dacians.

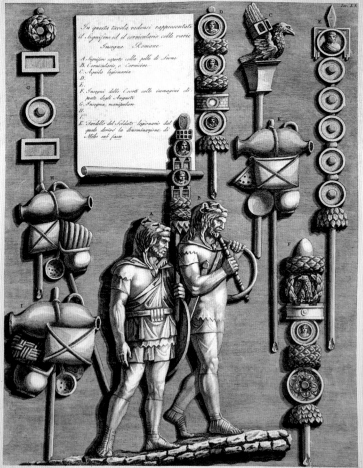

Etchings by Giovanni Battista Piranesi with details from Trajan's Column.
BAR Collection

Top: Roman military standards – two legion eagles, three signi and one Victoria vexillum. Details of scene XXVI, where legions cross a mountain river after the Battle of Tapae. On the right, covered, a signifer or standard bearer.

Bottom: a signifer and a cornicen, who sounded orders and signals, both wearing animal furs over their armor. Details of the marching equipment carried by legionaries and of standards of other Roman units.

return loaded with war spoils, but they failed to block Rome's supply lines.

Similar diversionary attacks were never carried out again. Some historians believe that a punitive expedition was launched against the rich *davae* and Dacian cities on the Siret River that Romans suspected to be part of the coalition targeting Moesia. But there was little more than suppositions to justify this version. Romans had already built a *castellum* at Barboşi (today part of Galaţi on the lower Danube), next to a *dava* which is close to where the Siret flows into the Danube. Upstream from Barboşi, another dava thrived at Poiana (in Galaţi county) by maintaining long-standing trade relations with the Greeks and Romans in Dobrogea. Either Poiana or Barboşi was the ancient *Piroboridava*, a settlement mentioned by geographer Ptolemeus, where Roman troops were garrisoned during the Dacian wars. Around 102, Romans also planned to erect advance camps (in today's Prahova and Buzău counties at Târgşorul Vechi, Mălăieşti, Drajna de Sus, Pietroasele) to oversee the settlements and mountains passes in this turbulent region.

Back to the Orăştiei Mountain Range

Meanwhile, Trajan went by land to one of the main Danube ports, Novae or Oescus, and from there he sailed upstream to Drobeta. Near the Orăştiei Mountain Range, after the 101 campaign had been interrupted by the cold season and the Moesia operation settled, Romans organized a new offensive against Dacia's strongholds. They used a complex strategy, with several armies converging from different directions into the deep north-to-south Grădiştea Valley. At least three armies advanced on the Dacian capital.

Given an absence of detailed records, it is difficult to trace a precise timeline of the military operations around the Sarmizegetusa center-of-power in 102 AD. The string of events proposed below is hypothetical, based mainly on archaeological finds and the few descriptions made by Cassius Dio and less on the scenes depicted on Trajan's Column.

The trench-lines surrounding marching camps built by the Romans during their offensive suggest that the attack was launched from mountain-top plateaus from several

Grădiştea Valley, southward view towards the Orăştiei Mountains and the village of Costeşti

directions. In order to destroy the Dacian fortifications, Romans avoided the deep valleys bordered by forested hills and traveled mainly on relatively flat ridge trails offering strategic advantages. From these alpine meadows, Legions were able to move in several directions without climbing or descending too much. They thus had excellent visibility and could stay out of valleys. The route was one least expected by the Dacians who planned their defensive in anticipation of attacks from valley approaches. On high-ground, the risk of a surprise attack was considerably lower and Romans had a dominant or at least equal position to that of their enemy. However, reaching the top meant considerable effort for the legionaries, who had to carry heavy equipment and build large camps, each surrounding several thousand men and animals, organize water supplies, pull up the tents, and so on.

To coordinate such complex troop movements on such a large area, Romans needed an efficient network of messengers. No records have been left about the way commanders communicated, but a well-devised system must have been in place, employing well-trained soldiers and maybe locals who knew the terrain.

Most probably, two Roman armies came up from the Streiului Valley (an easy access to Hațeg Country). One of them left the valley turning leftward at Pui village, where a marching camp may have existed. The mission of this force was to conquer the plateau now occupied by the village of Târsa. The well populated Dacian settlement at Târsa was flanked by two important Dacian protective citadels, Piatra Roşie and Blidaru. To take hold of it, one had to seize Blidaru and the nearby tower system, taking control of the whole area south and south-west of Sarmizegetusa and of one of the main access ways to the capital. Following this plan, Romans started their ascent towards Fizeş and Cioclovina, two high elevation villages. Several barrier fortifications were found along this route, indicating that Dacians tried to halt or at least delay the Roman advance. A very strong fortification awaited the Romans above the Ponorici karst valley.

The following step was to besiege and destroy Piatra Roşie. Undoubtedly, the troops built a camp to organize their siege, as they had in front of every other major Dacian stronghold. The camp had not been found because no archaeological digs were carried out in the civilian settlement below the citadel. We have no idea how the hypothetical siege went. Once they overtook the plateau and burned down the Dacian village, Romans built a camp on the other end of the plateau, towards Blidaru. Vague traces of the camp are still noticeable today near the Târsa church.

More strategically, the Romans wanted to launch their siege from the high-ground meadows in order to avoid the steep hills and fortified towers that surrounded Blidaru on the side of the Grădiştea Valley, as the fortified system of isolated towers and the citadel were much more difficult to conquer from the valley only. The towers were probably left to the army approaching from the north – as we shall see later on.

Close combat scene between a Roman auxiliary soldier and an unarmored Dacian warrior, inspired by Trajan's Column.

Four kilometers (2.4 miles) separate Tàrsa from the citadel on an easy, even descendent slope. The only obstacles facing the Romans were the towers on a hill named La Vămi, in the proximity of the citadel. This is where the sanctuaries of Pietroasa lui Solomon were destroyed. Ravaging Dacian sanctuaries was an essential step as a way of chasing their gods away or convincing to them to abandon the Dacians.

The siege of the well-positioned and high-walled Blidaru fortress, however well equipped with Roman-style artillery (*balistae*) was quickly settled. The Dacian strongholds were not devised for heavy siege supported by machines and engineering works. Suffice it to say that its water reservoir was outside the walls. Inside the walls, the 100 or 200 men could not have lasted long despite buried food vessels discovered by archaeologists. Piatra Roşie or Căpâlna were in the same situation. It does not mean that fighting was easy or that Dacians did not defend their places fiercely, especially since all the citadels were equipped with the latest military techniques and defended by professional soldiers. Huge sacrifices must have been made by both sides.

(Continued on page 120)

Military defenses in the Orăştiei Mountains. *Dacians cut the forest to erect barrier fortifications but also to have better visibility on enemy movements. Behind, a wooden palisade and a roofless tower with an artillery platform. In the background, a mountain-top Dacian citadel built in stone. Detail from scene LXII.*

Romans set fire to a Dacian barrier fortification with a wooden tower and palisade. *In the background, behind hilltops, a massive group of Dacians carrying two dracones. Detail of scene LIX. The digitally added colors are purely hypothetical.*

Barrier fortification at Ponorici

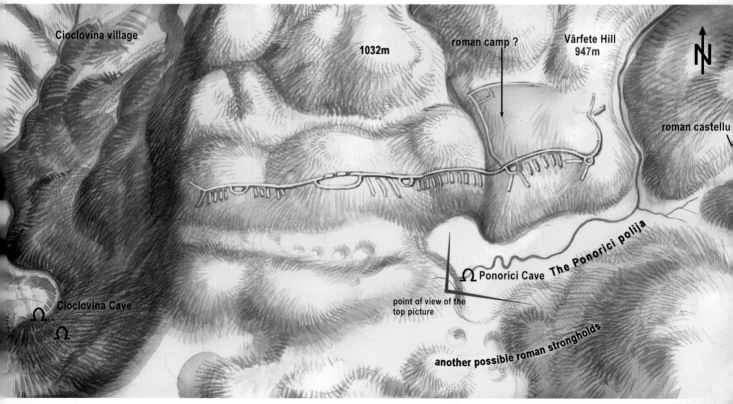

Cioclovina village

1032m

roman camp ?

Vârfete Hill
947m

N

roman castellu

Ponorici Cave

The Ponorici polija

point of view of the
top picture

Cioclovina Cave

another possible roman strongholds

roman Castellum ?

The Ponorici depression and the Ponor stream meandering towards the cave (at the base of the steep ravine hidden by the path in the foreground). Traces of the barrier fortification were found on the left-side hill (see the arrows).

BARRIER FORTIFICATIONS AT PONORICI CIOCLOVINA

Traces of barrier fortifications were found between the middle valley of the Strei River and the citadels in Piatra Roşie, Blidaru and Grădiştea Valley. They were meant to block the access of a potential aggressor. The most impressive and visible of the fortifications is an earth, wood and stone wall almost 3 km (2 miles) long. It was built above the Ponorici valley and Cioclovina cave. The monumental defense was erected from massive tree trunks and woven twigs filled with earth plaster, that made two parallel walls 5 meters (15 feet) apart, but interconnected with beams. The filling – emplecton – was rammed earth and crushed stone, similar to the murus dacicus technique. The wall was higher on the valley side facing the enemy. On top of the wall ran a walkway protected by a battlement. Stretches of narrower walls came out of the fortification every 20-50 meters (60-150 feet), like the teeth of a comb. They ranged between 50-100 m (150-300 feet) and were intended to break the rows of the attackers. In other locations, huge round bastions allowed the wall to be protected from the side. Most researchers admit - under some reservations – that this fortification system was built in Decebalus' time, possibly after Domitian's wars.

Unfortunately, only few and superficial studies were conducted here and the role these fortifications played in the Dacian-Roman wars was left to speculation. The Cioclovina-Ponorici wall underwent massive fire, as indicated by the burnt clay and rocks still visible on the site.

Reconstruction of an attack against the Ponorici fortification. *In the foreground, a cornicen signals the orders of the centurion to the legionaries. The centurion holds the vine staff, a sign of his commanding position. In the background, a group of soldiers launch a testudo-formation attack against a part of the fortification destroyed by fire.*

Legions led by Trajan himself came up the Grădiştea Valley, coming down from the Mureş River to the North. The first fortress on their way was Costeşti. They built a *castellum* just below it, as a base for their siege.

The second army going up the Streiului Valley halted in front of the Băniţa citadel and blockaded until its occupants had to surrender. The fortress was completely destroyed and a garrison left behind. The Romans were now free to reach the mountain-top meadows and from there, following the relatively easy paths on the ridge, advance all the way to Sarmizegetusa Regia. We are not aware of any Dacian barrier fortifications placed in their way to hinder their advance. We only know that once they reached the top, they erected an impressive marching camp including earth ramparts and a palisade right under Jigorul Mare Peak.

From there, the army continued to the Comărnicel Saddle, where they made the junction with another column, as we shall see. Trench-lines of three Roman marching camps are still clearly visible to-this-day on the Comărnicel Peak. Two are rectangular and one almost octagonal, perhaps for animal and horse stables and supplies. One of the camps was built by a Legion moving eastward from Băniţa, the other by Legions marching northward across the mountains from Oltenia. These 102 AD invasion routes have been the object of long debates among specialists. It is now very difficult to separate the traces left in 101-102 from the ones left in the second campaign to unfold three years later in 105-106. Archaeologically speaking, one cannot tell

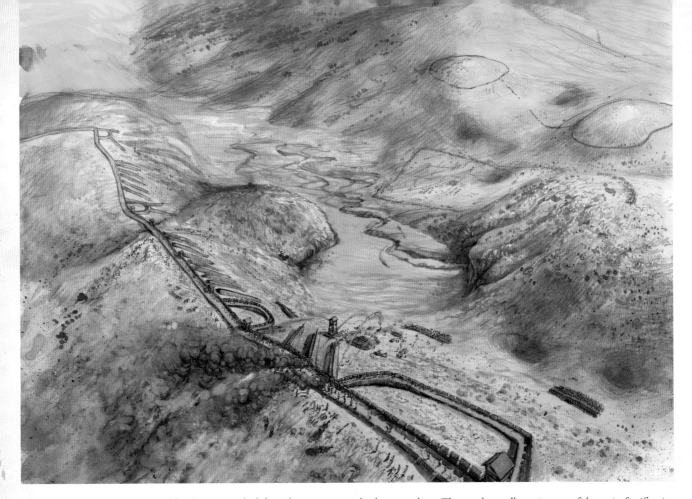

Seen from above, the reconstructed battle scene on the left might appear as in the drawing above. The wooden walls coming out of the main fortification had the role of dividing the attackers into smaller groups. Some of them were directed obliquely towards the left, forcing them to expose their right flank. Bastions allowed defenders to come closer to the attackers. The complexity of this unique fortification made some scholars doubt that it was Dacian.

Three of the Dacian military objectives attacked and destroyed by (probably) the same Roman unit that followed the route Strei Valley – Pui village – Ponorici fortification - Piatra Roşie citadel – Tărsa –Blidaru citadel and towers.

Above: the impressive remains of the Ponorici wall, over 5-6 meters wide at the base and over 3-4 m tall. Red earth and calcined rocks confirm that the construction was destroyed by a huge fire.

Top right: Piatra Roşie hill and the top plateau where the citadel used to be.

Bottom right: the foundation of the isolated tower at "La Vămi".

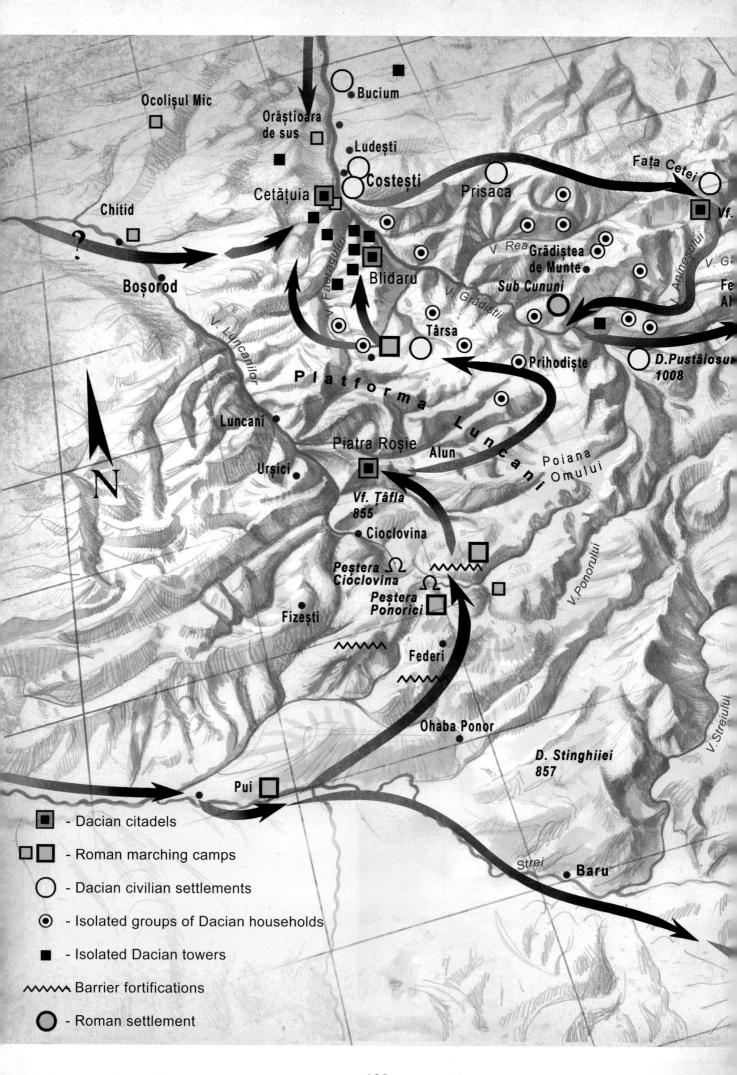

Ocolișul Mic

Orăștioara
de sus

Bucium

Ludești

Costești

Prisaca

Fața Cetei

Vf.

Cetățuia

Chitid

V. Rea

Grădiștea
de Munte

V. G

?

Blidaru

Sub Cununi

Fe
Ah

Boșorod

V. Făcăragului

V. Grădiștii

Târsa

D.Pustâiosu
1008

V. Luncanilor

Prihodiște

P l a t f o r m a

L u n c a n i

Luncani

Piatra Roșie

Alun

Poiana
Omului

Urșici

Vf. Țâfla
855

Cioclovina

Pestera Ω
Cioclovina

Ω

Pestera
Ponorici

V. Ponorului

Fizești

Federi

Ohaba Ponor

D. Stinghiiei
857

V. Strejului

Pui

Strei

Baru

N

- Dacian citadels

- Roman marching camps

- Dacian civilian settlements

- Isolated groups of Dacian households

- Isolated Dacian towers

- Barrier fortifications

- Roman settlement

Reconstruction of a carroballista used by Dacians during a siege. A part of this artillery weapon was found in the Costeşti citadel. Skulls and standards are war trophies, as shown on the Column. So is the Roman helmet worn by one of the warriors.

the difference between camps built three years apart. A difficult problem was to decide whether an army or even two could indeed attack from the southern high-ground of the mountains. Apparently they did.

The recent discovery of a marching camp[13] right

13   Information from Dan Oltean (see the bibliography).

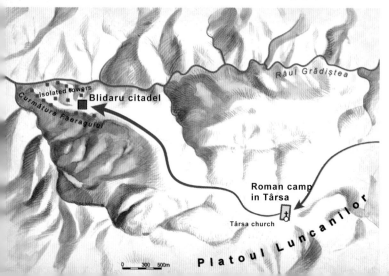

under the Parâng Peak, at over 2,300 meters altitude (6,900 ft), suggests a dramatic scenario: troops crossing the Carpathians from south to north, from Bumbeşti (Gorj county) to Comărnicel Peak close to Sarmizegetusa. Ancient armies had boldly ventured across the mountains before, if we were to think of the expeditions led by Alexander the Great, by Hannibal or by Caesar, who crossed the Alps.

At least two Roman camps are known at Bumbeşti, north of Târgu Jiu, close to the place where the Jiu River flows out of the mountains. A third is uncertain. They all could have been used as starting points for crossing the mountains. But there were two ways to get

The location of the Târsa Roman camp (near the church) and its position and location in relation to the Blidaru citadel. The red arrows indicate the Romans' main direction of attack.

Blidaru citadel, bird's eye view *(2011). The whole area between the Costeşti and Blidaru citadels, including the Grădiştea Valley hillsides, were fortified by a complex of isolated towers. Five of them were lined-up only on Curmătura Faeragului hill. Photo: Nicholas Dimăncescu*

to Bumbeşti. One was through Drobeta (three camps known on the route) and another starting at the Danube River and going up the Jiu River. Romans could have started from Oescus-Sucidava, downstream from the Jiu-Danube confluence. In this case, they would have paused at the very large camp in Răcari (Dolj county), which would explain its size and position. Both routes could have been used, even during the same expedition. From Bumbeşti, at least one massive column of legionaries did go up the eastern slopes of the Jiu Valley forcing a passage over the 2,500 meters high Parâng Mountains and building the marching camp we mentioned earlier on a peak named Coasta lui Rus at 2,300 meters, west and above the source of the

Lotru. Other marching camps remain unidentified. The next known camp on this route is on Pătru's Peak (2,100 m high), built after the crossing of the eastern Jiu Valley and still visible today. Then, after another day of marching, the southern group could reach the junction point on the Comărnicel Peak. The three camps there were able to shelter many thousands of legionaries. Convoys of mules loaded with barrels provided daily water needs (or sour wine sweetened with honey) for soldiers camping at Comărnicel. Such strongly situated base camps allowed the Romans to impose a total blockade against Sarmizegetusa.

Meanwhile, the army column presumably led by Trajan finally conquered the Costeşti fortress after an

(Continued on page 128)

Panorama of the Băniţa Valley facing the north-east of the Orăştiei Mountains *(Şureanu), with two of the routes probably taken by Roman armies. On the right, units coming from Oltenia over Parâng (a route proven by the recently found marching camp on Rus' Ridge). On the left, the group coming up from Băniţa citadel (already besieged and burnt down). Adapted after Dan Oltean. Photo: Dan Oltean.*

Reconstruction of the two rectangular field camps on Comărnicel Peak. (See satellite view on the following page.)

FIELD CAMPS

The system of marching camps built in the alpine meadows of the Orăștiei Mountains was a result of efforts to conquer the Dacian citadel and is unique to Dacia. The location of these forts highlights the Roman strategy and directions of attack. They used mountain-top trails and took advantage of superior marching conditions on almost horizontal plateaus along the alpine range. This offered wide visibility and prevented ambushes and surprise attacks. All camps were built on dominant high-ground with wide horizon views. Judging by their location, they were probably used during one warm season, probably the spring of 102 AD. At that altitude, winters were extremely harsh, with snowstorms and freezing temperatures, so spending the winter there was out of the question.

The outline of these field camps trenches remained unaltered over time, as no one came to build on top of them, as it happened in more sheltered places.

Most marching camps still visible on the mountain tops around Sarmizegetusa are four sided and have rounded corners. Geography forced some to take irregular shapes, such as an obliquely cut corner at Rus' Ridge, or the octagonal shape on Comărnicel Saddle (some researchers doubt this third camp was actually Roman). Temporary camps were protected by fortifications placed either in front of the entrances (titulum), or inside, curving leftwards. The barrage fortifications consisted of a ditch

A field camp is erected on a mountain top. Showing stone walls is a mere convention (like many other artistic licenses on the Column) used to help read the story. Detail from scene LXV.

and an earth and stone wall. The top of the wall was reinforced with a palisade – one row of stakes. The troops slept in large leather or canvas tents.

Unfortunately, the shape of the camps may only be discerned from the air. Seen from the ground, they don't seem to have any relevance. The two large camps on Jigorul Mare Peak (1500 m/4,500 ft) and on Pătru's Peak (2,100 m/6,300 ft) are still very visible from above. Another marching camp was recently discovered on Rus' Ridge (2,300 m/6,900 ft). Many others are barely distinguishable or even uncertain, requiring further research to prove their existence.

Many such field camps were identified around the Dacian citadels, some abandoned as soon as the wars were over (the mountain top ones), others living on in a more permanent form (in stone). Some of the latter are: the camp at Orăştioara de Sus, 6 km (10 miles) downstream from Costeşti; the castellum at the foot of the Cetăţuia Hill in Costeşti; a camp whose traces are visible behind the old school on the Luncani-Târsa plateau; at least one camp adjacent to the wall in Ponorici-Cioclovina, erected after the Dacian fortification fell; the camp on top of the Muncel Hill; and the fortification built in the middle of the Dacian capital after the conquest.

Left: Mules carrying barrels of water and wine to supply the numerous troops on the mountains. Roman soldiers also had ratios of posca (a mixture of vinegar and water, flavored with plants and sweetened with honey). Detail from scene LXII.

Right: Marching camp on Jigorul Mare Peak. Oblique aerial view taken in February 2011. Photo: Nicholas Dimăncescu.

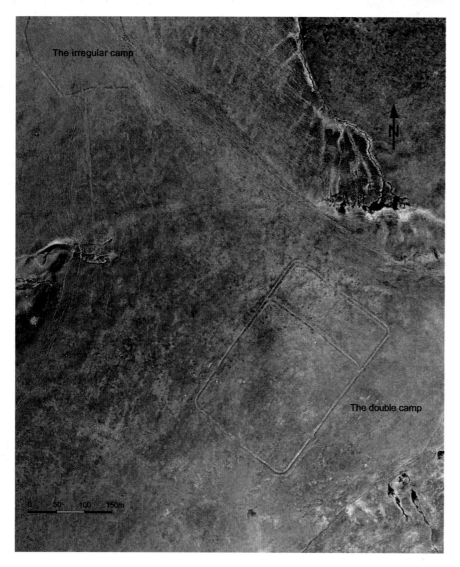

The irregular camp

The double camp

The double camp on Comărnicel Peak, in a satellite view. *The two north-eastern sides indicate that at some point, probably during the same 102 campaign, the camp was enlarged by a third to accommodate extra troops. On the left upper corner, one may notice part of the irregular enclosure of the third, octagonal camp. Source: INIS Viewer (geoportal.ancpi.ro)*

Marching camp on Jigorul Mare Peak. *Aerial view of the north-eastern corner. The wall and the ditch are still very visible almost 1,900 years later. The corner is cut by a shepherds' trail. Photo: Dan Dimăncescu*

exhausting siege. Archaeologists found a fragment of an artillery weapon inside the citadel, confirming that the Dacians used ballistae, largely the same as the Romans. Trajan's Column confirms it. Afterwards, the same army probably joined the Târsa legions to help destroy the isolated tower system in the Costeşti-Blidaru area. Unfortunately sparse details hardly allow one to understand the terrible battles and dramatic moments that unfolded in the mountains. The Column is a victor's bias intended to flaunt Roman successes while minimizing the setbacks.

Descending from the north and thus avoiding the narrow and dangerous Grădiştea Valley, Romans occupied the citadel on Hulpe's Peak and the still unexplored fortification above the Anineş Valley. The settlement at Faţa Cetei, where numerous man-made terraces have been identified, was burned. Although it's clear that the area was densely populated in ancient time, the absence of research and the thickly forested terrain surrounding it prevent developing more complex scenarios.

The besiegers could have encountered other Dacian fortifications blocking their way, like earth and wood ramparts, some backed up by artillery towers, as shown on the Column. At the confluence between the Anineş River with the Grădiştea River, the slopes of Vârtoapele Hill, once covered with artificial terraces, are home to the diminutive village of Grădiştea de Munte just a few kilometers below Sarmizegetusa. Here, in a place named "Sub Cununi" (Under the Crowns), superficial archaeological digs came across the traces of a Roman settlement inhabited until at least 175 AD (dated by an inscription). The remains of Roman mortar masonry, the coins and the two tombstones found here indicate it had a stable population. This is where Trajan may have organized his headquarters to coordinate the military operations and after the war is could have become a permanent Roman settlement, meant to keep an eye on the area over a longer term.

When it comes to the siege of Sarmizegetusa, details are missing, too. Archaeological research is incomplete (or incompletely published). Was the fortress strong enough to require a siege? We don't know for sure. Maybe it was. The Roman military units coming here on mountain trails were well-trained legionaries, specialized in siege engineering and machines. We can see them on the Column, erecting their mountain-top camps represented - unrealistically perhaps - as made of stone. Trajan's Column shows violent battle, siege scenes, and massacres at the end of the first war. One sees siege towers, ballistae and covered siege ramps. Infamous Moor cavalry are shown as fighting around the capital, led by Lusius Quietus, a Moor prince from Mauritania (today Morocco) naturalized in Rome and one of Trajan's best

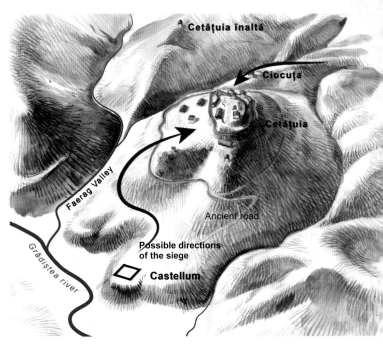

Siege of the Costești citadel. *Location of the Roman castellum built on a terrace under the citadel and two possible directions of the attack.*

Preparations for a siege in the mountains. *While two Dacian aristocrats give up to Roman pressure and abandon Decebalus (on the left, in front of Trajan), legionaries erect wooden structures for the siege. In the background, one may see another camp (of course, a field camp made of wood and earth) with ballistae installed on the walls. Scene LXVI*

Decebalus organizes his defense in the mountains. He has gathered all the available warriors to protect the capital. The Dacian king has also brought barbarian fighters like Sarmatians from the east and Germans from the west to his side. Diplomacy has failed. Trajan has decided to destroy the Dacian capital and sacred temples. And Dacian gods seem to have abandoned Sarmizegetusa. Decebalus' helmet is reconstructed after those sculpted on the base of Trajan's Column. So are the draco standards, with their heads in beaten bronze sheet and their bodies in colored canvas. Vertical animal-head trumpets, like the Celtic carnyx, were used by Dacians to send acoustic signals in battle.

generals. The fearsome Moors formed light cavalry units famed for mastering attacks on difficult terrain and for daring tactical movements[14]. They are represented on the Column in two scenes in their characteristic exotic appearance: dreadlocks curled like sheep wool, dressed in a tunic and riding saddle-less, armed with only a round shield and two spears. Dio Cassius succinctly records their vital contribution:

"Lusius, attacking (the Dacians) in another quarter, slaughtered numbers and captured still more alive." (68, 8, 3)[15]

At the same time, Dacian ambassadors and peace envoys appear. Cassius Dio's Roman History unfortunately contains too little and imprecise information in this part of the war: *"Undertaking to ascend the heights themselves, he secured one crest after another amid dangers and approached the capital of the Dacians [...]*

---

14 It's very unlikely that Moors were the engineers and users of the mountain camps like those at Comărnicel or Hulpe's Peak, as speculated in older literature. The camps were built by the same legionaries who also organized the sieges – work that was not delegated to auxiliary troops.

15 English translation by Herbert Baldwin Foster, Project Gutenberg License.

Decebalus had sent envoys even before his defeat, not the long-haired men this time, as before, but the noblest among the cap-wearers. These threw down their arms, and casting themselves upon the ground, begged Trajan that, if possible, Decebalus himself should be permitted to meet and confer with him, promising that he would do everything that was commanded; or, if not, that someone at least should be sent to agree upon terms with him. Those sent were Sura and Claudius Livianus, the prefect; but nothing was accomplished, since Decebalus did not dare to meet them either, but sent envoys also on this occasion. Trajan seized some fortified mountains and on them found the arms and the capture engines, as well as the standard which had been taken in the time of Fuscus. Decebalus, because of this, coupled with the fact that Maximus had at this same time captured his sister and also a strong position, was ready to agree without exception to every demand that had been made — not that he intended to abide by his agreement, but in order that he might secure a respite from his temporary reverses. So he reluctantly engaged to surrender his arms, engines and engine-makers, to give back the deserters, to demolish the forts, to withdraw from captured territory, and furthermore to consider the same persons enemies and friends as the Romans did, and neither to give shelter to any of the deserters nor to employ any soldier from their empire; for he had been acquiring the largest and best part of his force by persuading men to come to him from Roman territory. This was after he had come to Trajan, fallen upon the ground and done obeisance and thrown away his arms. He also sent envoys in the matter to the senate, in order that he might secure the ratification of the peace by that body. After concluding this compact the emperor left the camp at Zermizegethusa, and having stationed garrisons here and there throughout the remainder of the territory, returned to Italy. "The envoys from Decebalus, upon being brought into the senate, laid down their arms, clasped their hands in the attitude of captives, and spoke some words of supplication; thus they obtained peace and received back their arms. Trajan celebrated a triumph and was given the title of Dacicus..." (68, 9, 10)

Decebalus' capital and the Dacians religious center - Sarmizegetusa Regia – was surrounded. A settlement

The deadly Moor light cavalry, riding bareback, leads bloody battles in the forested valleys of the Orăştiei Mountains. Scene LXIV

Complex battle scene in the Orăştiei Mountains.
Dacians counterattack in force. Two warriors shoot a ballista from the top
of a wooden fortification. Romans order the auxiliaries into the battle: Balearic slingers,
Syrian archers (on the left, among the trees). Dacian tarabostes fight valiantly with their curved falces. Second part of scene LXVI

at Feţele Albe, on an adjacent hill, was overtaken by the armies pouring down from the mountains. The foot of Muncel Hill was covered in Roman troops arrived from the Anineş Valley. And the main Roman army – that had arrived via the Comărnicel Peak – launched an attack from the *castellum* on top of the Muncel. They were charging the least fortified side of the Grădiştea Hill. After bitter fighting, Sarmizegetusa was conquered. The Dacians key stronghold and spiritual sanctuary had fallen. Civilians, craftsmen – especially ironsmith - ran away, hiding their tools and hoping to return and get them back sometime. Hundreds of terraced houses were burnt to the ground. Elaborate temples were demolished and a strong Roman garrison was quartered in the former capital, as confirmed by both archaeological evidence and by Dio Cassius. Emperor Trajan had achieved his main goals.

It's hard to understand why former researchers of Trajan's Column and the Dacian wars could not accept the idea that Sarmizegetusa was conquered at the end of the first war (in 102), when it was obvious that this had been the main goal of the Roman expedition. From Constantin Daicoviciu on, historians adopted the very unlikely theory that Decebalus and Trajan made a truce and signed a peace treaty before the Dacian capital was occupied. What was, then, the purpose of Trajan's expedition to Dacia?

The peace ceremony, as sculpted on the Column, was entitled *deditio in fidem* "surrender in good faith." It meant capitulation under the terms set by the victor and forced the latter to show magnanimity. The act of capitulation was a ceremony in which the defeated placed his life, family, subjects, weapons, possessions and even gods at the mercy of the Roman Emperor and people. The Column shows a large group of warriors with their weapons thrown on the ground, their hands stretched in supplication towards the Emperor. Two Dacian aristocrats kneel down while a third touches

Battle scenes become more frequent of the Column towards the end of the first war. *They are all related to the Orăştiei Mountains confrontations, but it is very difficult to make a precise identification of each location. The first scene shows a Roman auxiliary troops attack. Beside the soldiers wearing the typical equipment of auxiliaries, on may identify a Balearic sling-thrower, a bare-chested Suebae warrior and six oriental archers in the background, wearing high helmets with scale neck guards. Four Dacians barely withstand the Roman attack while others flee in a hurry, leaving six dead bodies behind. The Dacian fortification is an interesting detail. It almost certainly represents one of the numerous wood and earth barrages thrown in front of the invaders (some unexplored earthen walls lay across the Muncel Hill, in the western quarter). The gate tower with the entrance passage turning right has an artillery platform instead of a roof, allowing Dacians to use bows and ballistas against arriving enemies. The following scene, separated from the former by a tree, shows another violent fight under the walls of a citadel. Dacians abandon the fort while Roman legionaries in their **lorica segmentata** and yielding rectangular shields advance in a **testudo** ("turtle") formation. This is one of the clearest and most beautiful representations of this fighting formation in the whole of Roman art. We may assume it is the siege of Sarmizegetusa. Scenes LXX and LXXI.*

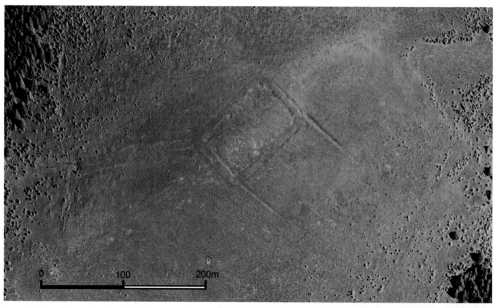

0   100   200m

__The Roman camp on Muncel Peak__ (1,560 m/4,700 ft), above Sarmizegetusa Regia. Barrier fortifications descending in lines from this fort controlled access to the capital. Judging by the shape and location (see the drawing of the Muncel Hill above), we believe the camp was used by Romans as a base to attack and siege the Dacian from above. Satellite view: INIS Viewer, geoportal.anepi.ro.

Trajan's knees in a gesture of prostration and humility. It is unlikely that this should be Decebalus, although Dio Cassius wrote that the Dacian King threw himself at Trajan's feet. Almost certainly, the King is the dignified *tarabostes* standing behind the kneeling noblemen. Trajan must have showed *clementia* and *humanitas* – generosity and benevolence - towards his enemy.

This act meant that Decebalus not only did not share the fate of Vercingetorix, the Gaul King captured by Caesar, locked up in Rome and cruelly killed during public festivities. Rather, he was spared humiliation and allowed to keep his royal standing.

Trajan could have captured Decebalus, but he did not, considering it was wiser to show him mercy and generosity. He needed the Dacian King to remain a friendly subject of Rome and a stabilizing and respected regional leader. These must have been the diplomatic calculations Trajan made as the first war came to an end.

Roman legionaries conduct engineering works for the siege of Sarmizegetusa. In the foreground, soldiers cut trees for buildings and to allow better view during the attacks. The tower made of horizontal tree trunks could be an observation post or a siege tower. The representation is standardized and simplified.

After his return to Rome in December 102, Trajan received the title of *Dacicus*, conqueror of the Dacians. The peace conditions were particularly tough. All conquered territories became part of the Empire. The peace treaty required that Dacians abandon their citadels after dismantling them under Roman supervision. Romans garrisons replaced the fortifications. The annexed territory was probably limited to the Banat, Oltenia and Haţeg Country, all the way to the Sibiu Depression. Romans did not go beyond the Mureş River, or at least they had not left any garrisons there. Decebalus was sent away from his capital and forced to find another seat outside the Roman area.

SARMIZEGETUSA REGIA AFTER THE CONQUEST

After the systematic destruction of all the fortifications and buildings and sanctuaries in Sarmizegetusa, Romans built an earth and wood camp on the ruins of the Dacian citadel. The traces of this first camp (because as we shall see, two consecutive forts were erected there) are barely visible today, so it's only in recent years they started to be studied. And since the site holds fragments of temporary earth fortifications

that could be both Dacian and Roman, or even used by both sides at different moments, reconstructing a timeline is extremely difficult. The Roman intervention was massive. The legionaries built or modified several terraces in the central area in order to build their camp, baths and residential buildings.

At the first Roman settlement, erected in 102, archeologists studied the remains of a Roman ironsmith workshop, which was built on the foundations of a Dacian mint shop. During the second Dacian war, the garrison here was probably attacked by the Dacians and chased away. In 106, Romans came back with their mind set to build a stronger fort able to withstand any future Dacian threat. Units (*vexilla*) from Legions II Adiutrix, VI Ferrata and IIII Flavia Felix started building a stone citadel. In the wall next to the gate towers, which were made of wood, limestone blocks bore the names of the participant legions[16]. On the terrace right below, a thermal bath used the same water supplies as the Dacians had – a couple of sources half a kilometer away. The new wall cut through the old Roman ironsmith shop in the earthen fort.

16 Roman soldiers used to inscribe the name of their units on the materials used to build the camps.

The impressive capitulation of the Dacians. *The whole Dacian elite, weapons laid on the ground, is forced to submit to the Roman eagle and to Trajan. In the background, we may see the walls of what is probably Sarmizegetusa and complex siege works such as wooden ramps (agger) and covered galleries. On the right, in another scene, we may see Dacians forced to destroy their fortifications. Scenes LXXV-LXXVI.*

This is the citadel we can still see on Grădiştea Muncelului – the one that the public long believed to be Dacian. Although the wall is built with Dacian stone blocks taken from the terrace walls of the Sacred Area, from the paved road or from other structures, the building technique is completely different from *murus dacicus*. The rounded corners of the enclosure, the two opposite gates, the shape, the absence of Dacian towers (the foundations of two small towers were found, but they were completely different than Dacian specific ones), everything points out to a Roman military camp, widened in the lower part to include terraces IV and V (see the plan on p. 139). Inside, traces of several Roman wooden barracks were found, including one built with mortar (an exclusively Roman technique). Why didn't Romans use mortar for the walls of their new camp, but only resorted to re-using the remains of the Dacian citadel, in a rough imitation of *murus Dacicus*? Probably because they had huge quantities of finely cut stone at hand and the Dacians blocks hardly needed any mortar. Or maybe in order to complete the walls as soon as possible. The walls of the baths were built with mortar, a sign that they were erected later, in no rush.

Initially, the archaeologists who unearthed this camp thought Romans did nothing else but re-build a Dacian citadel destroyed by the siege. However, no sign of an older Dacian fortification were found underneath. The Roman camp seemed to be the first construction on that site. Inside it, again, no trace of stone or wooden Dacian buildings, except for a water reservoir dug in the ground and of a mint shop (mentioned earlier) right under the wall. However, some historians believe that the top terrace of the Roman fort, at 1.000 meters altitude, was at some point guarded by a small square enclosure, a Dacian fortress destroyed by the Romans (see p.63). This theory advanced by archaeologist Ioan Glodariu from Cluj is based not on clear evidence (there are no drawings or photos), but merely on the summary description of traces found on the rocks. Such a fortification would only make sense as an early phase of the Roman fort (a *castellum?*). Until clearer evidence is found, a Dacian fortress on top of the "nipple" at Grădiştea Muncelului is merely hypothetical. The only certain fact, accepted by all archeologists, is that the citadel is a Roman camp, slightly atypical in shape but certainly built by legionaries.

Aerial view of the Sacred Area of Sarmizegetusa Regia in 2011. Photo: Dan Dimăncescu

Many traces of Roman dwellings were found outside the fortification, in the Sacred Area. Unfortunately, the recording of the findings made by Constantin Daicoviciu were not considered important. At the time, the priority was the mysterious and unknown Dacian civilization. Until recently, there was very scarce information about the Roman presence at Sarmizegetusa Regia, because the communist regime didn't consider it politically correct. The digs on the 10th terrace after 1989 showed that Romans had completed important works there: they leveled and widened a new terrace, the 9th, and erected a silo (the source of the burned wheat grains that were considered to be Dacian). The 10th terrace held

Roman houses, at least one of which was decorated with mosaic. After a fire during the Roman period, the terrace was leveled for a second time. It is unclear for how long Romans stayed here and when they left Sarmizegetusa. Lower, in the village of Grădiştea de Munte, in the place named "Sub Cununi", a small Roman settlement allegedly survived for at least 60 years after the 106 conquest.

Limestone blocks with inscriptions found in the wall of the Roman camp at Sarmizegetusa Regia. They were carved by legion soldiers who built the fortification, probably right after 106.

Left: *Leg[io] VI Ferrata*
©MNIT– Cluj Napoca
Right: *Leg[io] II Adiutrix P[ia] F[idelis]*
Photo: Iosif Vasile Ferencz ,
©MCDR –Deva.

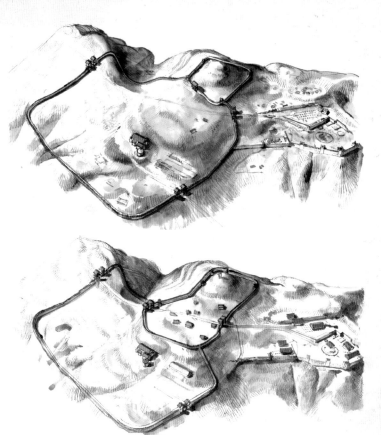

Right: *Two possible scenarios for the Roman fortifications Sarmizegetusa Regia after 102 (top) and after 106 AD. In the 102 stage, we assume that if a small stone fort did exist around the tip of the hill, it was a Roman one.*

Bottom: *Plan of the Grădiştea Muncelului site, completed and corrected with the traces noted on the aerial scan (LIDAR: Light Detection and Ranging) made in 2011 by Dan Snow and Sarah Parcak, authors of the BBC documentary "Rome's Lost Empire". Note the regular shape of the Roman camp on the upper side and the way its lower wall follows the limits of the terraces. Târsa camp (unpublished research) has a similar shape. Roman field camps of irregular shape are common in Europe; they were mainly located in conflict areas around the frontiers of the Empire.*

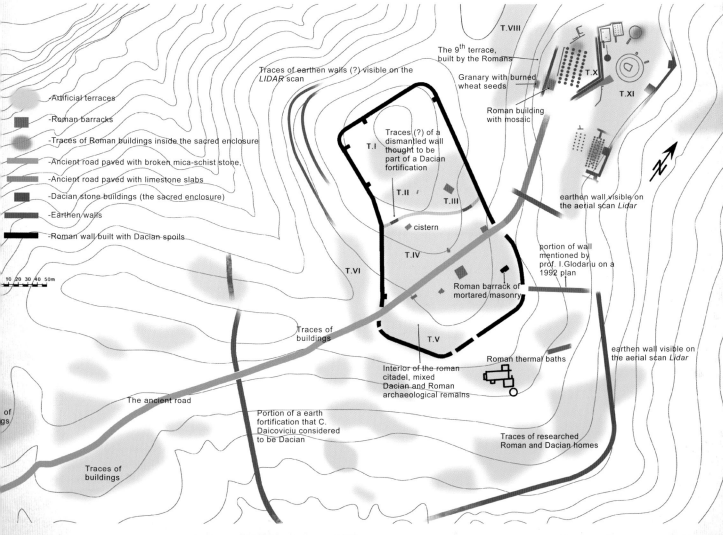

- Artificial terraces
- Roman barracks
- Traces of Roman buildings inside the sacred enclosure
- Ancient road paved with broken mica-schist stone,
- Ancient road paved with limestone slabs
- Dacian stone buildings (the sacred enclosure)
- Earthen walls
- Roman wall built with Dacian spoils

10 20 30 40 50m

Traces of earthen walls (?) visible on the *LIDAR* scan

The 9th terrace, built by the Romans

Granary with burned wheat seeds

Roman building with mosaic

T.VIII

T.X

T.XI

Traces (?) of a dismantled wall thought to be part of a Dacian fortification

T.I

T.II

T.III

earthen wall visible on the aerial scan *Lidar*

cistern

T.IV

portion of wall mentioned by prof. I.Glodariu on a 1992 plan

T.VI

Roman barrack of mortared masonry

T.V

earthen wall visible on the aerial scan *Lidar*

Roman thermal baths

Traces of buildings

Interior of the roman citadel, mixed Dacian and Roman archaeological remains

The ancient road

Portion of a earth fortification that C. Daicoviciu considered to be Dacian

Traces of researched Roman and Dacian homes

Traces of buildings

of gs

TRIUMPHAL MONUMENTS FROM ADAMCLISI

In 109 AD, an imposing triumphal monument was inaugurated in Moesia Inferior on a high-rise plateau visible from afar, somewhere between the Danube and the Black Sea. It was one of the largest memorials of a military campaign ever to be erected by the Roman army. In a nearby valley, on the site of an old village of the Getae, Trajan decided to found a Roman settlement named after the monument: Tropaeum Traiani. The settlement would become a thriving city, territorial capital of the Roman administration and Episcopalian seat after the rise of Christianity. It would fall under the attacks of Avar and Slavic forces, after being ransacked countless times in the late 6th and early 7th centuries. The ruins of the city, unearthed and partially restored, are typical for the period of Constantine the Great (with some reconstruction in Justinian's time, in the 6th Century).

Today, the monument stands near the village of Adamclisi in southern Dobrogea. The place bears a name of Turkish origin, also connected to the monumental ruin: *Adamclisi* comes from *Adam Kilisse* (*adam* for *man* and *kilisse* for *church*, meaning "The Church of Man").

Fragments of the Roman camp wall at Sarmizegetusa Regia, *long presented as a Dacian citadel, possibly repaired by the Romans. The wall is in no way similar to* murus dacicus, *although the blocks it's made of are Dacian.*
Top: *portion of wall near the western gate. Wide, rough construction erected in haste.*
Bottom: *andesite cylinder base from the great Sanctuary on the 10th terrace, reused by Romans for the wall of their camp.*

Dacian handcuffs found *by archeological looters (around 1995-1996) near the Piatra Roșie citadel (the item is part of the so-called "Piatra Roșie Deposit").*
© *Collection of the Hunyad Castle Museum, Hunedoara*

Tropaeum Traiani – *A metope shows the Emperor crushing the barbarian enemy under the hooves of his steed, a political message carried by a conventional image also used on coins.*
Photo: Stelian Petrescu, BAR Collection

Aerial reconstruction *of the three triumphal monuments of Adamclisi.*

The enormous compact masonry ruin looks like a dome and the locals used to believe it was an ancient church.

Few people are aware that the ruins of two other monuments stand near the Tropaeum. This includes a memorial altar or mausoleum and a circular funerary monument, the so-called "tumulus" (or maybe an older *tropaeum*?). Experts suggest that the two edifices, now practically invisible, were built from the same stone and with the same technique but at some time before the great triumphal monument. However, inscriptions on the central tower leave no doubt as to when the latter was completed, i.e., 109 AD. For the former two, historians have different theories. Some believe that the altar and the tumulus were built in Domitian's time after he battled the Dacians. Others think that they were ordered by Trajan at the end of the first campaign of 101 to 102 in memory of the Moesian battles.

In the Hellenistic tradition, *tropaeum* (meaning trophy) was a monument erected on a battlefield to preserve the memory of the battle. In ancient times it was made like a cross of a tree trunk and a horizontal beam. It reminded one of a human shape and was usually dressed in armor and adorned with weapons captured from the enemy, but it could also be made of stone. The Romans inherited the custom but no longer placed the monuments on the battlefield. They chose to erect them in more visible places, to maximize the impact on public opinion. At triumphal festivities in Rome, wooden trophies were built and adorned with real weapons. Often, the sculptures on Roman trophies built in memory of barbarian wars only show Roman weapons (as is the case at Adamclisi) and not the weapons of the defeated enemy.

The most important part of the large Adamclisi monument was the trophy placed on top of the building: a tree trunk adorned with a Roman general's ornate armor coat, (*lorica*

Mausoleum (?), Tumulus (?)

Tropaeum Traiani

Altar / funerary mausoleum

musculata), a *gladius* with an eagle-head pommel, four shields, a Hellenistic parade helmet capped by a griffon and leg shields (*cnemide*). Three barbarian prisoners, colossal statues of a standing man with hands tied behind and two sitting women, are represented at the feet of the trophy. In a first phase, a 12.5 meter (40 feet) high mausoleum tower was built and the sculpted trophy and prisoners were placed on top of it (see illustration). Later, a cylinder of stone and mortar (*emplecton*) was built around the tower and covered in a *parament,* a face of finely cut limestone blocks. The *emplecton* survived to this day, long after the face of the wall fell down. The cylinder peaked in a conical roof decorated with a rigorous geometrical design of stone scales decreasing in size from the bottom to the top. Relief carvings of barbarian prisoners from at least three different ethnic groups, their hands tied behind their backs, decorated the crenellated parapet of the cylinder. The famous set of 54 metopes or panels, of which 49 remain, offered scenes of the Roman military campaign against the barbarian coalition.

*Legionaries honor their Emperor. They parade without their helmets and armors, only with shield, **pilum** and gladius. Metope from Tropaeum Traiani. Photo: Stelian Petrescu*

Trophy represented on Trajan's Column, at the end of the first Dacian war. After an etching by Giovanni Battista Piranesi, 18th century.

*Two **vexillarii** and a **signifier**, bearers of legions standards, parade in front of the Emperor. They have their faces turned towards the metope representing the Emperor. Photo: Stelian Petrescu*

Tropaeum Traiani as it looked in the 1930s. Photo: Stelian Petrescu

Tropaeum Traiani was dedicated to *Mars Ultor,* "Mars the Avenger", the protecting god of the Roman army. The inscription under the trophy, possibly on both faces of the central tower, clearly indicated that the monument was completed in 109 AD. Between 109 and 114, the city of Tomis minted several coins with Trajan's effigy and the Adamclisi trophy in a simplified form further confirm the dating.

The design of the Adamclisi tropaeum, the largest in all frontier provinces, was inspired by cylindrical funerary mausoleums built in Augustus' time. Although it was perfect in terms of engineering and decoration, the quality of sculpted reliefs and statues seems

In the first stage, the trophy looked like a mausoleum tower, probably similar to the nearby altar. That is when the statues were placed on the top: the trophy along with the Dacian prisoners. In a second stage, the cylindrical body was erected…

Bronze coins minted in Tomis *during Trajan's reign, with a simplified representation of the monument.*
© - MNIR Bucureşti

Reconstruction of the monument in its final phase, in 109. The metopes might have been painted: we don't know, because no one has looked for traces of paint on the reliefs.

rudimentary and naïve[17]. But this is particularly so when compared with the art on show in great Roman-era cities. The art on the trophy is typically provincial, very similar to other instances of artwork at the frontiers of the Empire.

The main purpose of the monument was to make an imposing statement on behalf of the Empire. The trophy is dedicated to the heroic and unstoppable power of the Roman army and Empire, under the rule of the Emperor. But here, on the borders, where official art stood in view of barbarian peoples, it carried a different message and served a different purpose than in Rome. The vanquished were represented bluntly, in humiliating postures, suffering the wrath of Rome. Prisoners sculpted on the merlons of the parapet were chained to trees, hands behind their back, showing nothing of the dignified melancholy of the captured Dacians that would appear in finely carved marble in Trajan's Forum. The renowned German scholar Conrad Cichorius came to the conclusion, supported by other historians, that the sculpted decorations of the trophy were

restored around 316 AD, over 200 years after the monument's inauguration. This coincided with the renaming of the completely rebuilt fortified city of Tropaeum Traiani as *Civitas Tropaeensium,* "The City of Tropheeans." Thus, although the monument was initially built by Trajan, it is possible that the sculpted

Section through the ruin of the trophy and proposed reconstruction of the face covering the massive masonry. This is also the restoration solution used in the 1970s.

---

17 Experts noticed that two teams of craftsmen worked on the sculptures. One provided higher quality decorations, being probably qualified sculptors from Tomis or some other Black Sea city. The second team was probably made of stone carvers or cutters, forced by the circumstances to work on the figurative reliefs.

Reconstructed inscription on the main side of the mausoleum. On the upper side, the letters [I]MP[ERATOR] are still visible; below: [TRI]
B*[UNICIA]* **POT***[ESTATE]. The following rows read: [IN HONOREM ET]* **MEMORIAM FORTIS***[SIMORUM VIRORUM]* / *[QUI PUGNANTES]* **PRO**
REP*[UBLICA]* **MORTE OCCUBU***[ERUNT]. Underneath, the name of an unknown general and his place of birth are mentioned:* **POMP***[EIS]*
DOMICIL*[IO]* **NEAPOL***[IS]* **ITALIAE, PRA***[...]. (See translation in the text).*
*Composite photo after Emilia Dorţiu – "***A few observations on the military funerary altar at Adamclisi***", Dacia Magazine no. V, 1961.*

part of the trophy and the statues atop were replaced during Constantine the Great's reign, when scores or maybe hundreds of stone cutters and artists worked on the reconstruction of the city.

The German scholar based his opinion on the significant differences between the military equipment used in Trajan's time and the items represented on the metopes, as well as on the iconographic differences. According to him, the craftsmen who redecorated the metopes, or even added some, combined equipment from Trajan's time with contemporary 4th century equipment. The same considerations apply to the representations of barbarians, who seem to be a mix of Germanic people and Dacians.

The Great Mound – the Tumulus (the first *Tropaeum*?) was the hardest of three to describe and categorize. It consisted of four concentric wall rings and one wooden ring. The outer ring measured 36 meters (118 feet) across. Some archaeologists believe it to be a tumulus or a monument for a Roman general killed in battle. Others describe it as an early trophy, built in Domitian's time and destroyed after the *damnatio memoriae*, sometimes in Trajan's time.

The altar/mausoleum is 255 meters (740 feet) away from the tumulus. There researchers found fragments of a monument that proved to be an altar or funerary mausoleum, contemporary to the former and aligned with it into a unitary concept. The altar was a square with a side length of 6 meters; a few steps led up to it. It was made of large limestone blocks and simply decorated.

An attempted reconstruction of the monument in 1897 by Gr. Tocilescu, Otto Bendorff and Georg Niemann only dealt with the rectangular volume of the base.

By analogy with other mausoleums in Africa, Asia or Gallia, it is more likely that the initial structure was a slender three-step tower at least 10 meter high, with a two-sided or four-sided tiled roof. A monumental inscription ran all around the base. Only fragments of the name of the emperor who ordered the monument were preserved, not

Hypothetical reconstruction of the mausoleum. Inspired by Roman tower-mausoleums in Tunis, Gallia and Asia Minor

enough to know whether it was Domitian or Trajan. The rest of the dedication was reconstructed and translated as "TO THE MEMORY OF THE BRAVEST MEN WHO FOUGHT FOR THE HOMELAND AND FOUND THEIR DEATH".

Most unique, perhaps, was the carving into stone of names and places of origin of at least 3,000 to 4,000 Roman soldiers with an unknown Roman general from Pompeii heading the list. The primary facade carried the names of praetorian soldiers and legionaries, while auxiliary troops were on the lateral sides. Researchers who studied the inscription determined that the altar and tumulus were probably erected following a battle against the Dacians or Sarmatians. With the little information gathered so far, it is difficult to establish which one and exactly when. As always, in such unclear cases, there are different opinions. Some scholars say the monument was built soon after the bloody Adamclisi battle in the first Dacian war, during the Moesia diversion of the Germanic-Dacian-Sarmatian coalition

in the spring of 102 AD. Other experts believe that the two older monuments were erected in Domitian's time, to commemorate the battles led by Oppius Sabinus or Cornelius Fuscus (or even other battles of which nothing is known). Because both Roman generals died in the war against the Dacians and the former possibly in Dobrogea, the second theory would seem to carry the most weight.

Shortly after the conquest in 102, a huge bridge designed by Apollodorus of Damascus is erected over the Danube, at Drobeta. *Two camps are built (or rebuilt) in stone at the two ends of the bridge: Pontes and Drobeta. Works advance fast because they are conducted by legionary engineers, disciplined, efficient and highly qualified for such works.*

Bibliography

ActaMN   Acta Musei Napocensis, Cluj-Napoca (din 1964)
BHAUT   Bibliotheca Historica et Archaeologica Universitatis Timisiensis
MCA   Materiale și cercetări arheologice, București (din 1953)
SCIV, SCIVA   Studii și cercetări de istorie veche, București (din 1950); Studii și cercetări de istorie veche și arheologie (din 1974)
                           StComCaransebeș Studii și comunicări. Muzeul Județean de Etnografie și Istorie Locală din Caransebeș
MNIR   Muzeul Național de Istorie a României (București)
BAR   Biblioteca Academiei Române
MNIT   Muzeul Național de Istorie al Transilvaniei (Cluj Napoca)
MDCR   Muzeul Civilizației Dacice și Romane (Deva)

Synthesis papers / Monographs / Sources

Radu Florescu, Hadrian Daicoviciu, Lucian Roșu, Dicționar enciclopedic de artă veche a României, Ed. Științifică și Enciclopedică, București, 1980

Vladimir Iliescu, Virgil C. Popescu, Gheorghe Ștefan (editori/coord.), Fontes ad historiam Dacoromaniae pertinentes / Izvoare privind istoria României, vol. I, Ed. Academiei R.P.R., București, 1964

Ștefan Pascu, Liviu Constantinescu, Cornelia Bodea (comit. de red.), România. Atlas istorico-geografic, Academia Română, Institutul de Geografie, Ed. Academiei Române, 1996

Constantin C. Petolescu, Dacia, un mileniu de istorie, Ed. Academiei Române, București, 2010

Mircea Petrescu-Dâmbovița, Alexandru Vulpe (coord.), Istoria românilor, vol. I, Ed. Enciclopedică, București, 2010

Constantin Preda (coord.), Enciclopedia arheologiei și istoriei vechi a României, vol. I, II, III, Ed. Enciclopedică, București, 1994–2000

Daco-Roman Wars

Vitalie Bârcă, Oleksandr Symonenko, Călăreții stepelor. Sarmații în spațiul nord-pontic, Ed. Mega, Cluj-Napoca, 2009

Radu Florescu, Ion Miclea, Decebal și Traian, Ed. Meridiane, București, 1980

Alexandru Madgearu, Istoria militară a Daciei post-romane (275–376), Ed. „Cetatea de Scaun", București, 2008

Dan Oltean, Regii dacilor și războaiele cu romanii, Editura Dacoromana, Deva, 2012

Florian Matei Popescu, The Roman Army in Moesia Inferior (teză de doctorat), Conphys Publishing House, București, 2010

Ștefan Alexandre Simon, Les Guerres daciques de Domitien et de Trajan, École Française de Rome, 2005

Eugen Teodor, Ovidiu Țentea (editori), Dacia Augusti Provincia. Crearea Provinciei. Articolele simpozionului MNIR 13–14 octombrie 2006, Ed. „Cetatea de Scaun", București, 2006

Eugen Teodor, Ovidiu Țentea (editori), Dacia Augusti Provincia. Crearea Provinciei, catalog de expoziție MNIR, Ed. „Cetatea de Scaun", București, 2006

Radu Vulpe, Columna lui Traian, Ed. Sport-Turism, București, 1988

Articles

Constantin Augustus Bărbulescu, Relațiile daco-romane la Dunărea de Jos în lumina cercetărilor arheologice (sec. I a.Chr.–I p.Chr.), rezumatul tezei de doctorat www.unibuc.ro/studies/Doctorate2010Noiembrie/

Doina Benea, Dacia pe Tabula Peutingeriana, în In memoriam Dumitru Tudor, Ed. Mirton, Timișoara, 2001

Doina Benea, Direcții romane de atac dinspre vest asupra regatului dacic, Simpozionul Internațional „Daci și romani. 1900 de ani de la integrarea Daciei în Imperiul Roman", Timișoara, 2006

Dorel Bondoc, Northern Danubian Bridge. Heads from Oltenia, from the First War of the Emperor Traian against the Dacians (101–102 A.D.), Simpozionul Internațional „Daci și romani. 1900 de ani de la integrarea Daciei în Imperiul Roman", Timișoara, 2006

Hadrian Daicoviciu, István Ferenczi, Adriana Rusu, Dovezi epigrafice referitoare la participarea legiunilor II Adiutrix și VI Ferrata la cucerirea complexului cetăților dacice din Munții Sebeșului, în Sargetia, XXI–XXIV, 1988–1991

István Ferenczi, Castrele de marș de la Ponorici (com. Pui, jud. Hunedoara). Fortificații romane până acum necunoscute din partea vestică a Munților Sebeșului, în StComCaransebeș, III, 1979

István Ferenczi, Considerații în legătură cu castrele de marș romane din partea centrală a munților Șurianu, în ActaMN, XVIII, 1981

István Ferenczi, Observații tipologice și comparative cu privire la castrele de marș situate în zona cetăților dacice din Munții Șurianului, în Sargetia, XVI–XVIII, 1982–83

István Ferenczi, Depresiunea Cernei Bănățene folosită pentru înaintarea unor trupe romane către Munții Sebeșului, în Sargetia, XVIII–XIX, 1984–85

Gelu Florea, Archaeological Observations Concerning the Roman Conquest of the Area of the Dacian Kingdom`s Capital, în ActaMN, 26–30, 1989–93

Gabriela Gheorghiu, Un *modiolus* descoperit în cetatea de la Costești-Cetățuie, în Angustia, 9, 2005

Ioan Glodariu, Itinerarii posibile ale cavaleriei maure în războaiele dacice, în In memoriam Constantini Daicoviciu, Cluj, 1974

Ioan Glodariu, Sarmizegetusa Regia durant le regne de Trajan, în ActaMN, 32, I, 1989–1993

Ioan Glodariu, Decebal în ajunul confruntărilor armate cu Traian, în Istros, X, 2000

Ioan Glodariu, La Zone de Sarmizegetusa Regia et les guerres de Trajan, în Studia Antiqua et Archaeologica, VII, Iași, 2000

Ioan Glodariu, Vasile Moga, Castrul Roman de la Vârful lui Pătru, în Apulum, XXV, 1988

Viorel Moraru, Opinii referitoare la funcționalitatea complexului defensiv dacic de la Ponorici, în Sargetia, XVIII–XIX, 1984–85

Viorel Moraru, Hristache Tatu, O nouă fortificație dacică în zona Ponorici, în Sargetia, XVIII–XIX, 1984–85

Viorel Moraru, Hristache Tatu, Posibile fortificații dacice din val de piatră și pământ la Pui și Federi (jud. Hunedoara), în ActaMN, 26–30, I/1, 1989–1993

Coriolan Opreanu, Castrul roman de la Grădiștea de Munte, în Ephemeris Napocensis, IX–X, 1999–2000

Coriolan Opreanu, The Topography of the First Dacian War of Trajan (A.D. 101–102): A New Approach, BHAUT – Bibliotheca Historica et Archaeologica Universitatis Timisiensis, vol. 2, 2000

Constantin Petolescu, La Victoire de Trajan en Mésie Inférieure, în Thraco-Dacica, XVI, 1–2, 1985

Florian Matei Popescu, Participarea legiunilor din Moesia Inferior la expedițiile dacice ale lui Traian, în Dacia Felix, Studia Michaeli Bărbulescu oblata, Ed. Tribuna, Cluj-Napoca, 2007

Dumitru Protase, Legiunea IIII Flavia la nordul Dunării și apartenența Banatului și Olteniei de vest la provincia Dacia, în ActaMN, 4, 1967

Dumitru Protase, Quand la capitale de Décébal est-elle tombée dans les mains des romains?, în Ephemeris Napocensis, VII, 1997

Hristache Tatu, Fortificații de la Porțile de Fier ale Transilvaniei, în Sargetia, XVI–XVII, 1982–83

Hristache Tatu, Viorel Moraru, Dispozitivul defensiv dacic de la Ponoriciu, în Sargetia, XVI–XVII, 1982–83

Eugen S. Teodor, Aurora Pețan, Alexandru Berzovan, Cercetări perieghetice pe Platforma Luncani. I. Târsa și Poiana Omului, în ESTuar nr. 1, aprilie 2013 (în www.academia.edu)

Călin Timoc, Noi date referitoare la canalul de navigație construit de Traian la Porțile de Fier, la Simpozionul științific național „Războaiele daco–romane din timpul lui Traian", Deva–Geoagiu Băi, 7–9 noiembrie 1996

Călin Timoc, Despre dirijarea navigației fluviale în zona Porților de Fier ale Dunării în epoca romană, în Simpozionul „In memoriam Dumitru Tudor", Bibliotheca Historica et Archaeologica Universitatis Timisienis IV, Timișoara, 2001

Călin Timoc, Die Friedensbotschaften der Daker an Kaiser Trajan zur Zeit der dakorömischen Kriege (Soliile de pace ale dacilor la Traian în timpul războaielor daco–romane), la Simpozionul Internațional „Daci și romani, 1900 de ani de la integrarea Daciei în Imperiul Roman", Timișoara, 2006

Getic / Dacian Civilization

Dinu Antonescu, Introducere în arhitectura dacilor, Ed. Sport-Turism, București, 1984

Dumitru Berciu, Arta traco-getică, Ed. Academiei R.S.R., București, 1969

Dumitru Berciu, Buridava dacică, Ed. Academiei R.S.R., București, 1981

Florea Costea, Dacii din sud-estul Transilvaniei înaintea și în timpul stăpânirii romane, Ed. C2 Design, Brașov, 2002

Ion Horațiu Crișan, Burebista și epoca sa, Ed. Enciclopedică Română, București, 1975

Ion Horațiu Crișan, Civilizația daco-geților, Ed. Meridiane, București, 1993

Hadrian Daicoviciu, Dacia, de la Burebista la cucerirea romană, Ed. Dacia, Cluj, 1972

Alexander Fol, Valeria Fol, The Thracians, Ed. Tangra TaNakRa, Sofia, 2008

Gabriela Gheorghiu, Dacii pe cursul mijlociu al Mureșului, Ed. Mega, Cluj-Napoca, 2005

Ioan Glodariu, Arhitectura dacilor, civilă și militară (sec. II î.e.n.–I e.n.), Ed. Dacia, Cluj-Napoca, 1983

Ioan Glodariu, Eugen Iaroslavschi, Civilizația fierului la daci, Ed. Dacia, Cluj-Napoca, 1979

Eugen Iaroslavschi, Tehnica la daci, Bibliotheca Musei Napocensis, vol. 15, Muzeul Național de Istorie a Transilvaniei, Cluj-Napoca, 1997

Ion Miclea, Radu Florescu, Geto-dacii, Ed. Meridiane, București, 1980

Ernest Oberländer-Târnoveanu și Cornel Ilie (coord.), Capodopere din patrimoniul Muzeului Național de Istorie a României, București, 2012

Zoe Petre, Practica nemuririi: o lectură critică a izvoarelor grecești referitoare la geți, Ed. Polirom, Iași, 2004

Aurel Rustoiu, Metalurgia bronzului la daci (sec. II î. Chr.–sec. I d. Chr). Tehnici, ateliere și produse de bronz, Bibliotheca Thracologica, București, 1996

Aurel Rustoiu, Războinici și artizani de prestigiu în Dacia preromană, Cluj-Napoca, 2002

Valeriu Sîrbu, Oameni și zei în lumea geto-dacilor, Ed. C2 Design, Brașov, 2006

Mioara Turcu, Geto-dacii din Câmpia Munteniei, Ed. Științifică și Enciclopedică, București, 1979

Articles

Vitalie Bârcă, Echipamentul și armamentul defensiv al geto-dacilor în preajma războaielor daco-romane, în Istros, VIII, 1997

Cătălin Borangic, Falx Dacica. II. Tipologie și funcționalitate, în Nemus, anii II–III, 2007–2008

Cătălin Borangic, Sica. Tipologie și funcționalitate, în Nemus, an IV, 2009

Borangic Cătălin, Marius Barbu, Cai și cavaleri în spațiul geto-dac. Istorie, pragmatism și legenda, în curs de apariție

Ioan Glodariu, Sistemul defensiv al statului dac și întinderea provinciei Dacia, în ActaMN, XIX, 1982

István Ferenczi, Unele aspecte geografice ale luptei de independență a dacilor împotriva romanilor (101–102; 105–106), în Sargetia, XIII (1977)

Daniel Spânu, Misterioasele descoperiri de monede și podoabe de aur dacice din secolul al XVI-lea, în Argesis, XV, 2006

Daniel Spânu, Brățările dacice ca simbol, în Arhitectura, 6, 2011

Daniel Spânu, Probleme ale genezei și restaurării cupelor de tip kantharos de la Sâncrăieni, în MCA (serie nouă), VIII, 2012

Karl Strobel, Dacii. Despre complexitatea mărimilor etnice, politice şi culturale ale istoriei spaţiului Dunării de Jos, I, SCIVA, tomul 49, 1, 1998

Alexandru Vulpe, La Nécropole tumulaire gète de Popeşti, în Thraco-Dacica, 1976

Dacian Fortresses and Settlements in the Orastiei Mountains

Constantin Daicoviciu, Cetatea dacică de la Piatra Roşie. Monografie arheologică, Ed. Academiei R.P.R., Bucureşti, 1954

Hadrian Daicoviciu, Constantin Daicoviciu, Sarmizegetusa, cetăţile şi aşezările dacice din Munţii Orăştiei, Ed. Meridiane, Bucureşti, 1960

Hadrian Daicoviciu, István Ferenczi, Ioan Glodariu, Cetăţi şi aşezări dacice în sud-vestul Transilvaniei, Ed. Ştiinţifică şi Enclopedică, Bucureşti, 1989

Ioan Glodariu, Vasile Moga, Cetatea dacică de la Căpâlna, Ed. Ştiinţifică şi Enciclopedică, Bucureşti, 1989

Oct. Floca, M. Macrea, N. Lupu, I. Berciu, Cetăţi dacice din sudul Transilvaniei, Ed. Meridiane, Bucureşti, 1966

Ioana A. Oltean, Dacia. Landscape, Colonisation and Romanisation. Routledge Monographs in Classical Studies, Routledge, London/New York, 2007

Valeriu Sîrbu, Nicolae Cerişer, Vasile Romulus Ioan, Un depozit de piese dacice din fier de la Piatra Roşie (sat Luncani, jud. Hunedoara), Bibliotheca Septemcastrensis, XV, Sibiu, 2005

D. M. Teodorescu, Cetatea dacă de la Costeşti: rezultatele generale ale săpăturilor arheologice, Tipografia „Cartea Românească", 1930

Articles

Cristian Călinescu, Conservarea, consolidarea şi valorificarea complexului arheologic Sarmizegetusa–Grădiştea Muncelului, în Revista Muzeelor şi Monumentelor, 1982

Constantin Daicoviciu et al., Studiul traiului dacilor în Munţii Orăştiei, în SCIV, I, 1950

Constantin Daicoviciu et al., Şantierul arheologic de la Grădiştea Muncelului, în SCIV, III, 1952

Constantin Daicoviciu et al., Şantierul arheologic de la Grădiştea Muncelului, în SCIV, IV, 1953

Constantin Daicoviciu et al., Şantierul arheologic de la Grădiştea Muncelului-Blidarul, în SCIV, V, 1–2, 1954

Constantin Daicoviciu et al., Şantierul arheologic de la Grădiştea Muncelului-Blidarul, în SCIV, VI, 1–2, 1955

Constantin Daicoviciu et al., Şantierul arheologic de la Grădiştea Muncelului, în MCA, V, 1959

Constantin Daicoviciu et al., Şantierul arheologic de la Grădiştea Muncelului-Costeşti, în MCA, VI, 1960

Constantin Daicoviciu et al., Şantierul arheologic de la Grădiştea Muncelului, în MCA, VII, 1961

Constantin Daicoviciu et al., Şantierul arheologic de la Grădiştea Muncelului, în MCA, VIII, 1962

Constantin Daicoviciu, Hadrian Daicoviciu et al., Şantierul arheologic dacic din Munţii Orăştiei (1960– 1966), în MCA, X, 1967

Constantin Daicoviciu, Hadrian Daicoviciu et al., Şantierul arheologic de la Grădiştea Muncelului, în MCA, X, 1973

Hadrian Daicoviciu, Addenda la „Aşezările dacice din Munţii Orăştiei", în ActaMN, I, 1964

Hadrian Daicoviciu, Le Sanctuaire A de Sarmizegetusa Regia, în ActaMN, 17 (1980)

Hadrian Daicoviciu et al., Cercetări în incinta sacră a Sarmizegetusei, în MCA, XIII, 1979

Hadrian Daicoviciu et al., Verificări în incinta sacră a Sarmizegetusei, în MCA, XIV, 1980

Hadrian Daicoviciu et al., Cercetări arheologice la Sarmizegetusa Regia, în MCA, XV, 1983

Hadrian Daicoviciu et al., Cercetări arheologice la Sarmizegetusa Regia, în MCA, XVI, 1986

Hadrian Daicoviciu, Ioan Glodariu, Un nou munte întărit cu ziduri: Feţele Albe, în Revista Muzeelor, VI, 1964

Hadrian Daicoviciu, Ioan Glodariu, Ion Piso, Un complex de construcţii în terase din aşezarea dacică de la Feţele Albe, în ActaMN, X, 1973

Hadrian Daicoviciu, Ioan Glodariu, Puncte de reper pentru cronologia cetăţilor şi aşezărilor dacice din Munţii Orăştiei, în ActaMN, VIII, 1976

István Ferenczi, Importanţa unor metale neferoase şi a unor minerale în procesul de formare a puterii dacice în Munţii Orăştiei, în Sargetia, XIV, 1979

István Ferenczi, Contribuţii la problema formării aşezărilor cu carater protourban la daci (cu privire specială la Sarmizegetusa-Basileion), în Apulum, XXV, 1989

Gelu Florea, Consideraţii privind unele aspecte ale locuirii dacice în Munţii Orăştiei, în Sargetia, XX, 1996–1997

Gabriela Gheorghiu, Cisterne descoperite în zona capitalei regatului dac, în Sargetia, 27, 1997–1998

Ioan Glodariu, Cetatea de la Căpâlna în sistemul defensiv al statului dac, în ActaMN, XX, 1983

Ioan Glodariu, Addenda aux „Points de repère pour la chronologie des citadèles et des établissements daciques des monts d'Orăştie", în ActaMN, 32, I, 1989–1993

Ioan Glodariu, Infrastructura sectorului de nord al terasei a XI-a de la Sarmizegetusa Regia, în Daco-Geţii, Deva, 2004

Ioan Glodariu, Adriana Rusu-Pescaru, Eugen Iaroslavschi, Florin Stănescu, Sarmizegetusa Regia, capitala Daciei preromane, în Acta Musei Devensis, Deva, 1984

Ioan Glodariu et al., Sarmizegetusa Regia (zona munţilor Orăştiei), jud. Hunedoara, în Cronica cercetărilor arheologice, campaniile 1983–1992

Ioan Glodariu et al., Sarmizegetusa Regia (zona munţilor Orăştiei), în Cronica cercetărilor arheologice, campaniile 1993–2009

Eugen Iaroslavschi, Opinii privind „soarele gète de andezit" de la Sarmizegetusa Regia, în ActaMN, 31, 1994, nr. 1

Eugen Iaroslavschi, Vestiges romains dans la zone de la Sarmizegetusa dace, în ActaMN, 32, I, 1989–1993

Eugen Iaroslavschi, Zona siderurgică din preajma capitalei statului geto-dac, în Daco-Geţii, Deva, 2004

Mihaela Strâmbu, Ioan Glodariu, O nouă propunere de reconstituire a sanctuarului A de la Sarmizegetusa, în ActaMN, XVIII, 1981
Liliana Suciu, Amenajarea și funcționalitatea spațiului în locuințele așezării civile de la Grădiștea de Munte, în Studii de istorie a Transilvaniei, IV, 2000

Roman Army / Civilization

Raffaele d'Amato, Graham Sumner, Arms and Armour of the Imperial Roman Soldier. From Marius to Commodus, 112 BC–AD 192, Ed. Frontline, London, 2009
Mihai Bărbulescu (coord.), Atlas-dicționar al Daciei romane, Ed. Tribuna, Cluj-Napoca, 2005
R. Brzezinski & M. Mielzarek, G. Embleton, The Sarmatians 600 BC–AD 450, Osprey Publishing, 2002
Duncan Campbell, Brian Delf, Greek and Roman Artillery 399 BC–AD 363, Osprey Publishing, 2003
Duncan Campbell, Brian Delf, Greek and Roman Siege Machinery 399 BC–AD 363, Osprey Publishing, 2003
Duncan Campbell, Brian Delf, Roman Legionary Fortress 27 BC–AD 378, Osprey Publishing, 2006
Duncan Campbell, Adam Hook, Siege Warfare in the Roman World 146 BC–AD 378, Osprey Publishing, 2005
Peter Connolly, Tiberius Claudius Maximus. The Cavalryman, Oxford University Press, 1988
Peter Connolly, Tiberius Claudius Maximus. The Legionary, Oxford University Press, 1988
Peter Connolly, The Roman Fort, Oxford University Press, 1991
Ross Cowan, Adam Hook, Roman Battle Tactics109 BC–AD 313, Osprey Publishing, 2007
Nic Fields, Adam Hook, Roman Auxiliary Cavalryman AD 14–193, Osprey Publishing, 2006
Flavius Iosephus, Istoria războiului iudeilor împotriva romanilor, trad. rom. de Gheneli Wolf și Ion Acsan, Ed. Hasefer, București, 1997
Adrian Goldsworthy, Totul despre armata romană, Ed. Rao, București, 2008
Florian Matei Popescu, The Roman Army in Moesia Inferior, Ed. Conphys Publishing House, București, 2010
Boris Rankov, Richard Hook, The Praetorian Guard, Osprey Publishing, 1994
Graham Sumner, Graham Turner, Roman Army. Wars of the Empire (Brassey's History of Uniforms), 1997
Titus Livius, De la fundarea Romei, vol. 5, cărțile XLI–XLV, trad. rom. de T. Vasilescu, Fl. Demetrescu, P. H. Popescu, Ed. Științifică, București, 1963
Ancient Warfare, revistă trimestrială (lb. engleză), colecția 2007–2010, Ed. Karwansaray, Nijmegen, Olanda
Cristopher Webber, Angus McBride, The Thracians 700 BC–AD 46, Osprey Publishing, 2001
Peter Wilcox, G. Embleton, Rome's Enemies 1, Germanics and Dacians, Osprey Publishing, 1982–1994
Martin Windrow, Angus McBride, Imperial Rome at War, Ed. Concord Fighting Men 6000, 1998

Trajan's Forum, Trajan's Column, Tropaeum Traiani – Adamclisi

Florea Bobu Florescu, Monumentul de la Adamklissi: Tropaeum Traiani, ediția a II-a revăzută și adăugită, Ed. Academiei R.P.R., București, 1960
Claudia Costantino (editor), Roman Forum, Palatine, Colosseum, ghid, Ed. Electa, Milano, 2008
Constantin Daicoviciu, Hadrian Daicoviciu, Columna lui Traian, Ed. Meridiane, București, 1966
Emilia Doruțiu, Some Observations on the Military Funeral Altar of Adamclisi, în Dacia, V, 1961
Alberto Lombardo, Vedute delle antichità romane attraverso i secoli, Palombi Editori & Il Nartece, Roma, 2004
James E. Packer, The Forum of Trajan in Rome: A Study of the Monuments, University of California Press, Berkeley, 1997
Charles Gilbert Picard, Les Trophées romains, Ed. E. de Boccard, Paris, 1957
Mihai Sâmpetru, Tropaeum Traiani, vol. II, Monumentele romane, Ed. Academiei R.S.R., București, 1984
Lucrezia Ungaro (editor), The Museum of the Imperial Forums in Trajan's Market, Ed. Electa, Roma, 2007
Marcello Vannucci, I Medici. Una famiglia al potere, Newton Compton Editori, Roma, 2006
Leonard Velcescu, Dacii în sculptura romană, Ed. Les Presses Littéraires, Saint-Estève, 2008

Articles

Dana Dan, Mars Geticus. Realitate istorică sau literatură?, în Ephemeris Napocensis, 2001
Vasile Lica, Frontierele regatului dac după pacea din anul 102, în Pontica, 1998

TABLE OF CONTENTS